THE NEZ PERCES
SINCE LEWIS AND CLARK

Idaho Yesterdays
A Series Edited by Judith Austin
Idaho State Historical Society

MISS S. L. McBETH

THE NEZ PERCES SINCE LEWIS AND CLARK

Kate McBeth

With an Introduction by
Peter Iverson and Elizabeth James

University of Idaho Press
Moscow, Idaho
1993

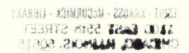

Originally Published in 1908
by Fleming H. Revell Company, New York
University of Idaho Press Reprint Edition 1993
Introduction by Peter Iverson and Elizabeth James
©University of Idaho Press, 1993

Idaho Yesterdays is a reprint series developed by
the Idaho State Historical Society and published by
the University of Idaho Press with
the assistance of the Idaho Centennial Commission

Cover design by Karla Fromm

97 96 95 94 93   5 4 3 2

Library of Congress Cataloging-in-Publication Data

McBeth, Kate C., 1832.
    The Nez Perces since Lewis and Clark / Kate McBeth ; with an
introduction by Peter Iverson and Elizabeth James.
        p. cm.—(Idaho yesterdays)
    Originally published: New York : F.L. Revell, 1908.
    ISBN 0-89301-160-6
    1. McBeth, Kate C., 1832. 2. Nez Perce Indians—Missions.
3. Missionaries—Idaho—Biography. 4. Presbyterians—Missions—
Social conditions.   I. Title. II. Series: Idaho yesterdays (Moscow,
Idaho)
E99.N5M2 1993
266' .51'092—dc20
[B]   92-29420
                                                        CIP

CONTENTS

ILLUSTRATIONS

INTRODUCTION TO
THE REPRINT EDITION OF
THE NEZ PERCES SINCE LEWIS AND CLARK

In October of 1877 Chief Joseph of the Nez Perce surren-
dered to United States Army generals Oliver O. Howard
and Nelson Miles. His reported words—"I shall fight no
more forever"—have echoed to the present. To many
Idahoans, Joseph's speech and the desperate flight of a
portion of his people before capture in the Bear Paw
Mountains of Montana encompass their acquaintance
with Nez Perce history. And yet, as *The Nez Perces Since
Lewis and Clark* suggests, Nez Perce life precedes and
follows those fateful days now more than a century ago.

Only two years after the Nez Perce War, Kate McBeth
arrived at the Nez Perce reservation in northern Idaho.
Her sister, Sue McBeth, already had resided there for six
years. Both were devout Presbyterians, inspired to come
westward by their commitment to missionary work.
Their efforts with the Nez Perce community continued
until the early 1900s during a time of continuity, change,
and challenge for the tribe.

In the past generation, national scholarly attention to
Native Americans has shifted away from an almost exclu-
sive fascination with the wars of the 1860s, 1870s, and
1880s. Recent scholarship has addressed the question of

Indian adaptation after the conclusion of armed conflict and the establishment of specific reservations. In taking a fresh look at federal policies as well as Native American efforts to build or rebuild economies, political systems, and societies, students are realizing anew both the power of imposed ideas and institutions and the resilient and incorporative nature of the Indians themselves. The issue for the latter was not simply whether to change or maintain all of the "old ways." Rather, as it has always been, the question was how to change. What could be grafted on to the tree of native life without uprooting a living, continuing entity?

Perhaps at no time in our history did Americans appear more convinced of the virtue and the efficacy of their social, political, and economic institutions than in the latter quarter of the nineteenth century. Railroad construction, massive immigration, urban growth, and the seeming conquest of Indian tribes and Indian lands all attested to the value of private property, public education, and individual opportunity. Most Americans perceived Christianity as an integral element in the success and prosperity of the nation.

Thus as immigrants streamed past Ellis Island and other points of disembarkation, bureaucrats, missionaries, and other agents sought to force Indians to be more like other residents of the United States. In fact the immigration model implied that if others could learn to speak a new language, learn new ways, and accept dominant national values, then Indians could, too. Indeed, until 1893 Presbyterian missionaries in the American Indian field worked under the authority of the Board of Foreign Missions rather than the Board of Home Missions. The McBeth sisters therefore arrived at a time of "Americanization" of American Indians. In Idaho and Arizona, Montana and New Mexico, native peoples heard the gospel of hard work, knowledge of English, and personal initiative. And they heard the Gospel, too.

Even as non-Indian farmers, ranchers, and miners sought access to or control over Indians' lands, philanthropists and reformers sought access to their minds, their beliefs, and their daily lives. Settlers and reformers proved an odd but brutally effective alliance in the years between the 1870s and the 1920s, although neither component particularly liked its association with the other. Two out of every three Indian acres were lost during this era. Indian parents, elders, children, and leaders all faced difficult questions about their future. It is not surprising that they did not always agree immediately with each other about the proper course to follow. Which church, if any, should I attend? Should my children attend school? Must I accept an allotment of land and, if so, where should it be located?

Because their own lives reflected change and assimilation, Sue and Kate McBeth had no doubt that the Nez Perce would embrace these elements. Born in Scotland in 1830, Sue McBeth emigrated to the United States as a young child; younger by three years, Kate McBeth was born in America. The McBeth family settled eventually in Wellsville, Ohio, and religion always formed a major part of their lives. Their society centered on the First Presbyterian Church of Wellsville, where Sue and Kate McBeth's father assumed the responsibilities of elder. Daily Bible readings attest to their strong religious convictions. The family's judgment overrode legal concerns with regard to the Fugitive Slave Act: the McBeth home served as a station on the Underground Railroad. Believing that God's will aided them in their endeavors to help free runaway slaves, Sue and Kate McBeth later attributed almost very event in their lives to that source. They had both been accepted in their teens as church members, and even the loss of their father a short time afterward could be attributed to the workings of Providence.[1]

The death of the McBeths' father nonetheless clearly and dramatically altered the course of the family. Sue McBeth now assumed leadership and responsibility for supporting her mother, three sisters, and a brother. Despite the hardships of supporting a fatherless family in the mid-nineteenth century, the two older sisters both managed to secure good educations, attending female seminaries in Wellsville and nearby Steubenville. Sue McBeth then convinced her younger sister to travel with her to Iowa, where they both taught for a time.

Kate McBeth returned to Wellsville and continued teaching in the area for the next few years. Sue McBeth, however, was destined soon to move west. She accepted a missionary teaching position on the Choctaw reservation in the Indian Territory (later Oklahoma). When the Civil War disrupted the workings of that mission, McBeth moved to St. Louis, where she worked for the United States Christian Commission caring for wounded soldiers. She had written in her diary in 1858, "I recalled the deep sympathy I felt [as a child] for the vanished race and longed to be a woman that I might go to the handful that yet remained and tell them the story of Jesus and try to show them the way to a home in heaven from which they could never be driven" (87). Her deep interest in Indian life soon surfaced once again, and in 1873 she accepted a teaching position on the Nez Perce reservation.

Although it begins with a general discussion of Nez Perce life in the early nineteenth century, *The Nez Perces Since Lewis and Clark* is primarily a tribute to the work of Presbyterian missionaries in that century: Marcus Whitman, Henry Spalding, and above all Sue McBeth. Published originally in 1908, the book takes the story of missionary efforts to the time of Sue McBeth's death in 1893. It almost goes without saying that Kate McBeth is not a disinterested observer of developments in Nez Perce country. From nearly the first page we can tell that this is the account of a Presbyterian of her day rather than a contemporary cultural pluralist. But if the contemporary reader can make her or his way past references to "a kind of devil-worship," "darkened minds," and "the old, dirty heathenism," then the book emerges as a rare first-hand rendition of certain dimensions of reservation life during a time of change.

Kate McBeth begins her story with the briefest of explanations about Nez Perce life before contact with the whites. Clearly she is not very interested in that world. Rather she uses it as a foundation for the first meeting of the people with the Anglo-Americans: the encounter with the Lewis and Clark expedition. To these explorers,

McBeth attributes little more than initial good will. Fur traders then gave the Nez Perces their first lessons in Christianity. According to the author, this acquaintance sparked curiosity and eagerness for conversion, leading to the fabled Nez Perce delegation of 1831.

As Francis Haines and other students of Nez Perce history have explained, the Nez Perces did not make the long trek to St. Louis specifically seeking the enlightenment of Protestant Christianity. Instead, they followed in the footsteps of a Spokane tribal member, known by the English name of Spokane Garry, who had traveled eastward to school and had returned in 1830 as the only Indian in the region with the remarkable gift of reading and writing. In an attempt to regain tribal prestige, in order to learn more about such powers as Spokane Garry had acquired, the Nez Perces dispatched four men to St. Louis.[2]

McBeth merely repeats a version of the widely accepted public belief that the Nez Perces came only in search of missionaries. This perspective we owe primarily to the elaborate version concocted by a creative, zealous man who did not even see the Nez Perces when they came to Missouri. William Walker, a recent visitor to the city accompanying a Wyandot delegation, perceived the Nez Perce journey as a plea for Protestantism and wrote so to New Yorker G. P. Disoway. Disoway in turn wrote an account for a missionary publication and the Nez Perces soon received their first missionaries.

Kate McBeth saw the trip to St. Louis as the most important event in Nez Perce history—not, of course, because the representatives sought social prominence or other benefits, but because they wanted missionaries. Even though McBeth misunderstood the reason for the journey, she does not misinterpret its significance. The Walker-inspired version influenced white perceptions of the Nez Perces for more than a century. From this point, then, McBeth traces tribal history through her natural focus: the efforts of the Presbyterian missionaries.

And there can be no doubt that the missionaries did play a major role in much of Nez Perce life during the 1880s. What McBeth does not do, however, is consider a wider range of issues, personalities, and developments that would give us a more complete and accurate image of the Nez Perce world. What we read about, generally speaking, is a simple dichotomy between "heathens" and Christians. There are few gray areas and the complexity of Nez Perce social or political organization is not presented to the reader. For example, in her discussion of the war of 1877, McBeth specifically points out that no Christian Nez Perces took part in the conflict. She thus implicates heathenism as responsible for the whole affair. However, as Alvin Josephy and other scholars have painstakingly demonstrated, the conflict resulted in part from the agreement Christian Nez Perces led by Lawyer—the head chief appointed by the government—had made reducing the reservation in 1863.[3] The Christian Nez Perces did not live in the portion of the tribal estate sacrificed by this agreement. By contrast, Joseph, White Bird, Looking Glass, Toolhoolhoolzote, and others lived in the area to be sacrificed. While McBeth shows sympathy for the non-treaty group for their exile to Oklahoma, she does not question the motives of the non-Indian residents or the government or Lawyer's group.

The troubling and crucially important matter of land allotment is also presented in a limited way. One chapter is entitled "The Allotment of Land," yet only a portion of it is devoted to the issue. The division of the tribal estate into individually owned parcels splintered many western reservations, including the Nez Perce. Those parcels were too small and often were leased to whites rather than farmed by the Indians themselves. Moreover, the "surplus" lands after allotment were also thrown open to outsiders. The Nez Perce reservation quickly became both reduced in size and fragmented in character. Allotment thus produced a lasting legacy whose consequences could not be perceived as fully in McBeth's day. To obtain a more detailed picture, the readers of this book will want to consult the letters of E. Jane Gay.[4] Cook, housekeeper, photographer, and companion for the allotment agent, Alice Fletcher, Gay provides us with a more candid assessment of divisions within the Nez Perces that were exacerbated by the division of tribal land. Of all the chapters in the book, "Fourth of July Camp Meetings Past and Present" may be the most cur-ious to a modern reader. The struggle over celebrations and church loyalties did not occur solely among the Nez Perces. On the Fort McDowell reservation in Arizona, similar disputes erupted over Fourth of July dances and observances. There another Presbyterian missionary, George H. Gebby, protested against a dance in the early 1900s. If allowed by the government, he alleged, "among these unmoral and half-civilized people it was often accompanied or followed by fights, jealousies and domestic difficulties."[5] This altercation helps us realize that the McBeths were hardly alone in their attitudes. In the same sense, the Nez Perces were not unique in attempting to find symbolic occasions to assert themselves. It is intriguing that on many reservations, two holidays of great symbolic importance—Christmas and the Fourth of July—were especially popular.

People employed as teachers or missionaries dispatched by denominations often thus found themselves caught up in controversies larger than they initially appeared. Not surprisingly, it could be difficult for teachers and missionaries to maintain cordial relations with all parties. They competed with parents for the attention and loyalty of the children in some instances; they competed with other missionaries for the souls of men and women. In an environment that they found isolated, in a climate that challenged their endurance, in housing that was modest at best, people such as Kate and Sue McBeth labored often for decades and usually in obscurity. Regardless of how one may judge their attitudes, one must acknowledge their dedication.

Such a description, to be sure, fits Indian agents as well. Even though they tended to move from one post to another with more frequency than did missionaries, they were also long-term laborers in the field. And at Nez Perce, Fort McDowell, and other reservations they too understandably saw themselves as unappreciated, underpaid, and overworked. Upon reflection, we can appreciate why an agent of firm views might clash with missionaries of an equally determined mind-set. This is just what happened between Agent Charles E. Monteith and the McBeth sisters.

Charles Monteith was the brother of John B. Monteith, the Nez Perce agent at the time of Sue McBeth's arrival in Idaho, and worked for his brother then as an agency clerk. Kate McBeth does not dwell on the matter, but her sister only served briefly as a teacher of the Nez Perces. Within a year, she had been transferred to missionary responsibilities. Apparently, John Monteith concluded that the older McBeth could not handle her charges. Haines tells us that she was "partly crippled because of some sort of paralytic stroke."[6]

By 1882, however, Charles Monteith himself served as the Nez Perce agent. Although Sue McBeth actually preferred teaching only theology, Charles Monteith never changed his views of her work after the initial disappointment. They feuded for years, with Kate McBeth of course joining on her sister's side. The McBeths viewed the agent as one who allowed and encouraged traditionalism; they railed against him from their bastion in Kamiah, sixty miles to the east of the agency at Lapwai—the latter a place Kate McBeth dismissed as a "moral cesspool."

Finally in 1885 Monteith wrote to the Commissioner of Indian Affairs asking that the McBeths be removed from the reservation. He claimed that they interfered with his authority and contended that inspectors for the Indian Service had recommended their removal. That summer

witnessed a flurry of charges, counter-charges, and inves-
tigations from both the Indian Service and the Board of
Foreign Missions.

During this time, Sue McBeth packed her belongings
and moved to Mount Idaho, just outside the reservation
boundary. In doing so she avoided the expected expul-
sion order. Kate McBeth was left in Kamiah to worry
on her own. Board of Foreign Missions director F. F.
Ellinwood traveled to the reservation and interviewed
several people about the McBeths, but he never talked to
them personally. After his return to the east, he issued
orders: Sue McBeth was to remain at Mount Idaho while
Kate McBeth was directed to move to Lapwai.

The move placated Monteith and, ironically, perhaps
served to improve relations between the sisters. Although
The Nez Perces Since Lewis and Clark is discreet on this
point, it is clear that Sue and Kate McBeth did not
always see eye to eye. Sue McBeth, as the older sister
and first arrival on the Nez Perce reservation, resented
Kate McBeth's presence in her domain and attempted
to control her activities—even to the extent of ordering
her younger sister not to allow women into her school
if they had not accepted Christianity. Even if she vehe-
mently disagreed at first, Kate McBeth eventually capitu-
lated. Separate locations gave each room to maneuver.

The personal conflicts between whites on the reservation affected Nez Perce lives. Surely the students of the
McBeths were influenced by the quarrels between the
sisters as well as their arguments with Monteith. The
break in the First Presbyterian Church of Kamiah is a

vital example. Deward Walker has written extensively about religious factionalism on the Nez Perce reservation, including the split in 1889 that established the Second Presbyterian Church of Kamiah. Walker notes that the division occurred after the McBeths left Kamiah.[7] However, they were at least partially responsible for it. Their support for Robert Williams, pastor of the First Presbyterian Church, over other ordained Nez Perce ministers fostered feelings of resentment and competition in the Kamiah community.

Kate McBeth saw the world of the Nez Perces in a very particular way. We may not agree fully with her world view, or we may be disappointed with her failure to address some topics. One wishes, for example, for more discussion of the Catholic mission at Slickpoo, more analysis of the effects of land allotment, more attention to the role and response to native religious leadership within Nez Perce Presbyterianism. On the other hand, *The Nez Perces Since Lewis and Clark* does help us to understand the mind-set of a missionary: the author reveals even more about herself than about the Nez Perces.

Devoted to her faith and to her students, Kate McBeth contributed to the Presbyterian legacy among the Nez Perces. As did the land-allotment work of Alice Fletcher, the McBeths had a significant impact on the lives of more than one generation on the reservation. While the Presbyterian Church does not command as large a percentage of the Nez Perce population as it did at the turn of the century, its continuing presence on the reservation attests to the work of the sisters long ago.

In an era when many despaired about the Indian present and the Indian future, the McBeths believed in what could be accomplished. For over forty years they learned something about the beauty of Nez Perce country and the determination of its people. A century after Sue McBeth's death, the Nez Perces remain on their land and remain a part of Idaho's future.

—Peter Iverson
  Elizabeth James

NOTES

1. The only published study of the McBeths is Allen Conrad Morrill and Eleanor Dunlap Morrill, *Out of the Blanket: The Story of Sue and Kate McBeth, Missionaries to the Nez Perces* (Moscow: University Press of Idaho, 1978).

2. Francis Haines [Sr.], *The Nez Perces: Tribesmen of the Columbia Plateau* (Norman: University of Oklahoma Press, 1955), pp. 51-62.

3. Alvin M. Josephy, Jr., *The Nez Perce Indians and the Opening of the Northwest* (New Haven: Yale University Press, 1965), chap. 10.

4. E. Jane Gay, *With the Nez Perces: Alice Fletcher in the Field, 1889-92* (Lincoln: University of Nebraska Press, 1981).

5. Gebby to Cato Sells, October 31, 1913, Record Group 75, Bureau of Indian Affairs, San Carlos Central Classified Files, 1907-1939, 111718-13-063, Salt River, quoted in Peter Iverson, *Carlos Montezuma and the Changing World of American Indians* (Albuquerque: University of New Mexico Press, 1982), p. 128.

6. Haines, *Nez Perces*, p. 3303. Apparently the stroke was triggered by word of Sue McBeth's fiance's death in 1870 (Morrill and Morrill, *Out of the Blanket*, p. 144).

7. Deward E. Walker, *Conflict and Schism in Nez Perce Acculturation* (Pullman: Washington State University Press, 1968; reprint Moscow: University of Idaho Press, 1991), pp. 67-69.

INTRODUCTION

THE following pages tell of the meeting of the old and new America on the western slope of the Rocky Mountains and picture the heroic lives of men and women of two races.

The story is set in a remote region and is concerned with persons whom the busy world rarely stops to consider. Nevertheless the impact here recounted, forms an essential part of the history of the northwestern portion of our country, while the spirit manifested in the actions recorded is fundamental to the highest individual and national growth.

Who are the Nez Perces Indians? The ethnographic problems of America are not yet solved. Over the land through the long years, man has been on this continent; many waves of migration have moved East and West; North and South.

At some time in the distant past, the linguistic family to which the Nez Perces belong, the Shahaptian, drifted along and settled between the Cascade Mountains to the west, the Bitter Root Mountains to the east, and the forty-fourth and forty-sixth parallels. Within this region occupied by their kindred, the Nez Perces seem to have clung to the eastern mountains and to have nested so long ago in the Kamiah Valley, that they claim this spot as their birthplace.

The Nez Perces are a mountain people, and the steadfast virtues of the mountaineer are theirs. Their native name, " Nim-e-poo," signifies " the men," or " the real people," an appellation commonly used by tribes to distinguish themselves from other peoples, upon whom they generally bestowed nicknames that characterized some peculiarity of dress or custom, as, the misnomer, Nez Perces, an example of a similar habit among ourselves.

In their ancient and native religion, the cosmic forces represented to the Nez Perces the power which gave them life. The wind was the breath of the universe, and as with our Aryan ancestors, it was the " gast," or ghost, the living force within, the breath of life.

The birds that sped through the air were the messengers between man and the invisible power above that animated all things. Crude as were their native beliefs, they were the results of a reverent outlook upon nature and a recognition that there was a power greater than man upon which he depended.

Over these simple beliefs, priest-craft with its love of power crept, in the guise of the " Te-wat," and the people through fear were constrained to unworthy practices.

But the vagaries of the magician could not wholly destroy the influence of the teachings of nature, as set forth in the orderly progression of day and night, summer and winter, and the regular movements of the heavenly bodies; nor could they silence the questions: Whence came I? What am I here for? Whither am I going?—questions, that wherever man has been found on the earth, he has been asking and seeking for the answer.

That these questions were haunting the thoughtful men among the Nez Perces, is evidenced by their determination to send a delegation to St. Louis to seek, after almost a generation had passed, the white traders who had come among them with compass and time-keepers and other mysterious devices that betokened knowledge, and to ask of them, light upon these ancient questions of man's life and destiny.

The four Nez Perces Indians so delegated, left their mountain home, carrying a burden that may be termed abstract, but which to them was far more real than the thousand miles of their weary march. The light desired came to the tribe at last but not by the hands of those who laid down their lives in the quest.

The occupation by the United States of the land west of the Rocky Mountains as a result of this remarkable journey is known to the world, but it has been left to Miss Kate McBeth to tell how the answer sought through that journey, finally reached the waiting Indians, and to reveal the nobleness of these people who were able to make so full a response to the high ideals set before them by their sanctified teachers.

When in 1889 I went to the Nez Perces Reservation, charged by the Government with the duty of carrying

out the provisions of the " Severalty Act," and to give
to each man, woman and child a share in their in-
herited tribal lands, I had the privilege of knowing
the Misses McBeth in the field where they had so
unselfishly laboured.

Much could be written of the wise way in which
they had builded, for they had sought to make the
individual strong, not only through his personal beliefs and hopes, but through his family life, and his
responsibility in the community.   He had been taught
Christian living as well as Christian thinking, and that
his life must be one in thought, in speech and in deed.

He had been instructed also in the history and laws
of our country.   So when the talk of allotting the
lands in severalty began, it became evident that only
among those who had been under the teaching of the
Misses McBeth, could the law be intelligently explained
and accepted.   The sisters had prepared their pupils
to understand the importance of citizenship to the
Christian Indians.

The only copy of the law under which the allotment
was to be made, that had ever reached the reservation, had been procured by a young Indian living in
Kamiah, and who became my interpreter during the
entire time of allotment.

The weeks spent in Kamiah by us were memorable.
The beauty and peace of the valley had in it more
than the merely pastoral quality ; it was pervaded by
the influence that had spread from the little cabin it

harboured. In this cabin, the Misses McBeth had
lived for years, bereft of comfort, exposed to cold and
to heat, forgetting themselves and ministering to
others. Here the elder sister battled with disease
and physical weakness and wrought her work within
the hearts of men, that widens with the years in its
far-reaching influence.

There, too, dwelt her pupil and coworker, Robert
Williams, a man of heroic mould. He was not gifted
with beauty of face or figure, but in manner he was
quiet and dignified, and when his serious face lighted
with a smile, it became beautiful in the revelation of
his gentle, loving soul. His steadfastness in what he
believed to be right; his clear-eyed faith that truth
must prevail; his unreserved forgiveness for wrong
done to him, were marked characteristics of the man.
These traits I have again and again seen magnified
under the cruel persecutions to which he was sub-
jected. He was a Christian leader, exemplifying in
his own life, the precepts he proclaimed from the
pulpit.

As I write, memories awaken of Colonel McConville, the vigilant, untiring friend and faithful officer,
with his gentle, resourceful wife; of helpers in the
field and in the school, giving unstinted service; and
of camping scenes with their touches of humour, their
queer devices, their manners, their pleasures, with the
constant labour and the perplexing task of adjusting
claims and settling disputes.

I hear again from a camp of Indians, halted for the
night on their way to the mines, their ponies laden
with garden produce to sell to the miners, the sound
of family prayer and song wafted over the hills as the
shadows fall and again the sounds in the early morning before they resume their journey over the mountain trails, float over to where I lie listening, nor can
I forget the courtly courtesies of Indian men and
women, nor their generous help and cordial support
in many a difficult experience.

The reasonableness of the Nez Perces Indians, their
willingness to look upon a new aspect of a subject,
their teachableness, and their patience were evidenced
during the four years I was among them. They have
gifts of mind and heart which cannot fail to make
them welcome as citizens of our common country.

The pathos, moral heroism and beauty of Christian
living and doing, pictured in this rarely interesting
volume, by the modest pen of the author, seem almost
to belong to another sphere, so untouched are they by
the selfishness and worldliness that jostle us at every
turn.

It is well to read of them, but better still to know
that they are true and remain with us as part of the
living forces within our land.

ALICE C. FLETCHER.

Peabody Museum,
Harvard University.

I

THE COMING OF LEWIS AND CLARK

Nez Perces History—Kamas—Kouse—First Dogs and Horses—
Homes—Te-wats—Sun Worship, Earth Worship—Lewis and
Clark's First Visit—Their Return the Following Summer—Story of
Wat-ku-ese.

IT is not easy to get much reliable history in that
indefinite, misty period lying between the settling of
the Nez Perces in the Kamiah Valley and the coming
of Lewis and Clark, about a hundred years ago. However, it is plain to see that this whole western coast
had been divided among the Indians. The Nez Perces
claimed all land lying between the Blue and the Bitter
Root Mountains. The Buffalo country, Montana, was
a common hunting ground—I might say, common
battle ground, where they were yearly destroying each
other. The Nez Perces and Sioux were always fighting. "Pe-sa-kul-kt" (cut-throats), is still the name the
Nez Perces give to the Sioux.

Compared with that of surrounding tribes, the Nez
Perces land was rich in its provisions for the people.
Its "kamas" and "kouse" fields were such broad
prairies, as the Weippe and Kamas prairies and the
region around Moscow. Those were their best root
countries. The Salmon, Snake, and Clearwater rivers
furnished fish, and the mountains game. The men

15

were responsible for the family meat, the women for the roots and berries, but in times of failure, or even scarcity, famine stared them in the face.   On the hunt it was days without food—then a feast.   It was espe-cially the industry of the women in digging and storing away for winter that kept them from feeling the pinch of poverty at any time.

Time was, when all the burdens were borne upon the people's backs.   How rich they felt afterwards, when dogs trotted along through the forests, carrying as much as fifty pounds each!   Brighter and better days came when they got a few horses from the Shoshones.   They were afraid of them at first, as in later years, of the cat, or " Pits-pits."   This was the sound to them of the word " pussy-pussy."   Much serious trouble grew with the multiplication of horses, for the Snakes, or Shoshones, were constantly skir-mishing around to steal their precious ponies.

Before going on the hunt, or to fish, a leader was chosen, to whom they were expected to give implicit obedience.   In their best days they had seventy-five villages, all on the banks of streams.   Each village had its chief or leader.   The head chief's village might be considered the capital of the group.   Vil-lages farthest up from the mouth of the stream were in danger from incursions of the enemy.   The upper village on the Snake was entirely destroyed, with the exception of two women and one man.   On the same river, near Asotin, lived a boastful man named Skin-a-way, who led out a band of six or seven hundred of his brethren against the Snakes, and not one ever returned to tell the tale.

They usually spent the winter months in their own pleasant valley homes, living in long houses built of sticks, grass, and skins, with a number of fires through the centre. The Indians spoke not of so many rooms in a house, but of so many fires. If the families were small, several families would use the same fire. There were no partitions, of course, for privacy. But of these long houses we shall hear a little further on.

Parents had little to do with the training of their children. If discipline was needed, the chief was appealed to. He had his band-whipper ready to administer the punishment which he decided upon. *The band supplanted the family.* This prevailed until the gospel came, when the bands were lost in the individual homes and families. The chief's power then began to wane.

During those early ages, whatever religion these people may have had to start with, had degenerated into a kind of devil-worship, in which the " Te-wats," or sorcerers, played a prominent part, with their enchantments, their dreaming, drumming, sleight-of-hand performances, and dancing. It is hard to classify their worship, mixed up with these abominations. There were many customs which must have come from the children of Jacob. Their chiefs were a kind of priests, who received the first-fruits of the land, and fish.   An unmarried man married his brother's widow. Indeed, no other book is so easy for these Indians to understand as the Old Testament.   " Oh, so we used to do ! " is often heard while they are studying it.

Sun worship and earth worship were started among them after the coming in of the " King George's men," or Hudson Bay Company.   Lewis and Clark's visit antedates this by several years.   Clark surprised three little Nez Perces boys, September 20, 1805, on the Weippe, their best " kamas " ground.   The boys ran and hid.   No wonder, for it was the first white face they had ever seen.   Lewis and Clark and company had just come in upon the Weippe from the Lo Lo trail—notwithstanding the statements of some that they crossed on the other trail.   They used both. The Nez Perces of to-day, if they want to cross the mountains, go out from Kamiah by way of Weippe on the Lo Lo trail, follow it for a distance—then strike across on the ridge to the Elk City trail.   Lewis and Clark came down off the hills above Oro Fino.   They met some of the people.   They were anxious to make canoes and pass down the river.   Right here a man met them, with a fine salmon, which he gave them for a present.   Either Lewis or Clark unrolled a package, tore off a red piece of cloth and bound it about the Indian's head.   That made him a chief forever.   Elder Billy, a trusted Nez Perces, thinks it was a piece of the flag.   This was above the north fork of the Clear-water, where the little town of Oro Fino now stands.

The people say that builders of the Northern Pacific Railroad took out the last stump left from the trees of which Lewis and Clark made their canoes. Lewis and Clark called these Indians the " Cho-po-nish." This was not correct, the word being " Chup-nit-pa-lu," or people of the pierced noses, or, again, in French, " Nez Perces."

The Nez Perces deny that they ever did, as a tribe, pierce their noses. Occasionally one would. They consider this name a misnomer, but Lewis and Clark must have had some reason for calling them " Cho-po-nish." The tribes of the Lower Columbia did pierce their noses. If the Nez Perces had any ornament in the nose, it must have been wampum.

Lewis and Clark did not find the Nez Perces naked savages, but wearing skin dresses. The women wore skirts reaching to the ankles ; the men's were shorter, with leggins and as many ornaments as they could find to bedeck themselves with. The finest was the bear's-claw necklace. The explorers did not much admire the Nez Perces disposition on first acquaintance, or, later, as they went down the river. They thought them selfish, avaricious, and so on, but upon their return in 1806, after camping among them for more than a month in the Kamiah Valley waiting for the snow to melt off the mountains, where they were treated as honoured guests, being given the best of their food, the fattest of their horses to slay and eat, they could not say enough in praise of the Nez Perces.

On the return from their journey to the sea, all the way up through Nez Perces land, Lewis and Clark were eagerly sought by the sick, the halt, the lame and blind, for in the previous autumn the explorers had kindly given medicine which had helped some of the Indians and so won for the whites a fame as wise doctors now.

At North Fork they were met by a delegation of Nez Perces to guide them on up to Kamiah, where already the principal men of the tribe awaited their coming. Couriers had been arriving daily in the Kamiah camp to tell just where the travellers were at a certain time and so calculating the time of their expected arrival.

On the 10th of May, 1806, Lewis and Clark had their first view of the beautiful Kamiah Valley. I am sure they saw no fairer scene in all their travels, carpeted then with grass and flowers, and on the other side of the Clearwater River the foothills enclosed by buttes rising each one higher than the other for several hundred feet. But pleasing as the scenery was, the interest centred in the village, a camp of Nez Perces. Their house, 150 feet long, was made of sticks, straw and dried grass. The twenty-four fires were placed in a straight line through the middle. All was excitement and bustle in the camp because of the expected guests. The younger women with their long fringed skin dresses, going to and from the Kamiah Creek, with their basket buckets for water, the older women hard at work pounding the kouse root into meal, in the stone mortars to make their bread. All day they had been looking towards the top of the mountain. There was no need of field-glasses for them, their eyes were trained to view things at long range. When the word " Wa-ko " (now they are coming) was heard, the grinders stopped to watch the descent. York, the black cook, was the greatest curiosity to the Indians. They even tried to wash the black off of his face. The white folk looked all about the same, so far as dress and colour were concerned. The travellers were willing to rest at short distances to make mental pictures of the scene.

Of course they were met at the foot of the hill by fine-looking braves on spirited ponies, who guided them to the entrance of the long house, where they were received in due form under the United States flag which had been sent in the previous fall to the great chief Black Eagle. Other important chiefs were there to assist Eagle in extending hospitalities to these honoured guests. No fear but that there was dignity enough in all this ceremony! Afterwards they were conducted to a spot already selected for their camp, where the chief had set up a large leather tent which he told them was to be their home as long as they chose to stay in the valley.

These white friends were not long in telling of their lack of food, and at once two bushels of kamas and other roots, with a dried salmon, were placed before them, for which the travellers were thankful. But the whites were not accustomed to living upon roots, and might become sick. So they proposed exchanging one of their poor horses for a fatter one in possession of the savages, which they might kill and eat.

The hospitable feelings of the Nez Perces chiefs were shocked at the idea of such an exchange and they replied, " The horses on all these hills are ours ; if you are disposed to eat such food, take as many as you like."   A young fat horse was soon brought and killed, and what a grand supper the strangers did have that first evening in Kamiah !   After the meal, they assembled the chiefs, smoked with them and explained the object of their journey.   There was but little sleep that night, for the Nez Perces were not sleepy.

The next day, May 11th, there was a great council of the chiefs.   Those present were Black Eagle, Hahats Ilp-Ilp, Red Bear, Cut Nose, Twisted Hair, Broken Arm and Speaking Eagle.   Who can at this date describe the dignity of that meeting, as the Nez Perces sat looking into the hearts of the white men before them ?   Think of the time consumed in communicating but a little information from one party to the other !   Lewis and Clark spoke first in English, to one of their men, who translated into French to Charboneau, and he translated it to his wife in the Minnetaree tongue ; she then put it into Shoshone and the young Shoshone into Nez Perces.   There was plenty of room for misunderstandings in such a process.

After the talk was ended, the spy-glass, the magnet, the compass, the watch, and the air gun were shown the Nez Perces. The fame of these wonders had reached them from the people of other tribes who had seen these things as the travellers passed through the year before.

The next day another council of chiefs alone was held to decide upon the answer to be given to Lewis and Clark. The chiefs had but one heart and said, "We trust them, we want their friendship, and the friendship of those who sent them. We will try to follow their advice and not go to war with other tribes, not even with the Shoshones."

After this decision all the people were called into the long house, where the pots were briskly boiling on the long row of many fires. Eagle was the first speaker, and explained to them the decision of the chiefs. He then rose and went from one pot to another stirring in meal made of kouse roots, all the while talking to the people, and concluded with an invitation to all who were ready to say " Ah " (yes), to their decision to come forward, partake of the food, while those opposed to it were to sit still where they were.

Of course all agreed and had a share in the mush, except the women, who tore their hair and wrung their hands in great distress, for they feared some snare for their people. No doubt they gave in and shared in the feast when the men arose and went out.

Lewis and Clark were more than a month there in the Kamiah Valley. Not all the time on the banks of the Kamiah Creek, they after a time moved just across the river, because the game was more plentiful there. Crowds of people came for medicine; even a good horse would be given in exchange for a bottle of eye-water.

It was June before they could get away, so long did the snow lay on the Bitter Root Mountains that year. Then the Nez Perces guided them out from the Weippe over the mountain trails into Montana, on the Lo Lo trail, the same trail upon which General Howard afterwards found so much difficulty in pursuing Joseph.

I have no difficulty in tracing the campings and the journeyings of these travellers all through Nez Perces land and in finding the evidence how the Nez Perces loved and trusted them! Their names are household words to this day. Just how much they trusted them can be seen by their following the white visitors' trail to the East, twenty-five years later, to have them explain some difficulties in the matter of religion. Oh! that visit! What a fertile subject it has been for camp-fire stories for more than one hundred years!

Here is one of their stories: Not long before the coming of Lewis and Clark, in some of the many battles in the Buffalo country, in Montana, a Nez Perces woman, Wat-ku-ese, was taken prisoner. The Indians who had captured her were returning to their own land, and on their way, they fought with another tribe, and the Nez Perces woman was again taken captive by the enemy, and so carried farther and farther away. It was while there, still a captive, that she saw the first white face that a Nez Perces had ever seen. We are inclined to think she was taken somewhere into the Red River settlement. Some time afterwards, with her child upon her back, she made her escape. Along the way she met with much kindness from the whites, whom she called the So-yap-po,—the crowned ones,— and by this name the white people are known among the Nez Perces to-day. They were called the crowned ones because of their hats. Her child died, doubtless because of starvation. She buried it beside the trail over in the Flathead country, where she was so fortunate as to find some of the Nez Perces, who brought her home, a poor diseased woman. She had much to tell about the strange people with white skins and light eyes who had been so kind to her.

Later, this poor woman was with the Nez Perces on their best kamas ground, the Weippe, when Lewis and Clark came over the Lo Lo trail and surprised them there. The first impulse of the Nez Perces was to kill them. Wat-ku-ese lay dying in her tent. She heard the talk about the strange people. She at once began to plead for them, saying, " Do them no harm. They are the So-yap-po, the crowned ones, who were so kind to me. Do not be afraid of them, go near to them." Cautiously they approached. The whites shook hands with them. This they had never seen done before, and in surprise said one to another, " They dandle us."   Wat-ku-ese died soon after, but she had lived long enough to keep Lewis and Clark from being killed by the savage Nez Perces. The fear of the white faces soon vanished and they became friends.

There are two events in Nez Perces history, so well known that even the children can tell about them. These are the coming of Lewis and Clark in 1805, followed by their return in 1806 from the coast; and the going out of the four in search of the truth about God, twenty-five years later.

II

SEARCH FOR THE LIGHT

Old Heathen Worship—Dissatisfaction with It—Rumours of a Book—
Four Nez Perces Sent to Search for the Light—Rev. Samuel Parker
and Dr. Whitman—Rev. H. H. Spalding and Wife the First Missionaries to the Nez Perces—First Station on Lapwai Creek—Buffalo
Tent—Mr. and Mrs. Spalding's School.

Up to the time of the coming of Lewis and Clark,
indeed, until after the coming of King George's men
(Hudson Bay Company) some years afterwards, the
Nez Perces did not have any idea of the worship of
God.   So if Lewis and Clark tried to direct their darkened minds into the light, it was at the time a failure;
but when afterwards, in their groping for an object of
worship, they began the sun worship, they recalled the
many gestures of Lewis and Clark upwards, as well as
those of King Goorge's men, saying to each other,
" Oh ! now we understand. They wanted to tell us
that the sun is God, and to worship him, but they had
no interpreter and we could not understand them.
Now we see. Now we know. The sun is our father,
the earth is our mother."

The Hudson Bay Company had a station for trade
in the Kamiah Valley, on the now " Kip-ka-pel-i-kan "
farm. The Nez Perces met the Hudson Bay Company
men at Colville, and also at Walla Walla. A sun-pole

27

was set up near the present site of Walla Walla.
There the Nez Perces met yearly for a great sun-
dance. Billy told me that many a time he had danced
around the pole, with great fear lest he should touch
it and die.

The mother earth shared in the honours with the
sun father. Their sun worship was at stated times or
feasts, as when the fish (salmon) came up and entered
the little streams in the spring, and when the first
spring roots (Se-with) were fit to eat. The head chief
or priest, would call the people of his group of villages
to worship. This was the Feast of First-fruits. No
one touched them until this ceremony was over, and
the chief or priest received first. The worshippers
with bowed heads formed a circle. The priest held up
a fish to the sun, turning in the direction the sun appears to move around the earth, all chanting as he
turned and turned—" Oh ! Father, bless the fish. Oh !
Father, bless us." This was their song. They then
dug a hole and placed the fish in it, covering it with
earth, chanting, " Oh! Mother, bless the fish. Oh!
Mother, bless us."

Other feasts were observed when the deer were
plenty, and when the berries were ripe. All worship
had dancing in it. In after years they were astonished
at their dullness in not understanding that the joyous
times that the Hudson Bay Company men wanted to
introduce among them, fourth of July and Thanksgiving, all meant worship.

The grace before eating was by turning the vessel around as the sun turns. The sun was consulted at all times ; before going out to hunt their horses, and before going out to hunt on the mountains. They never failed to acknowledge him as the great leader. All the products of the earth were his children, born of the earth. No wonder some of them, at the time of the Joseph war, " did not want to sell their mother, nor hurt her with a plowshare."

The Nez Perces were not long satisfied with the sun worship, for rumours were beginning to reach their ears that there was another, greater than the sun, who made both the sun and the earth. Whether they got this word first from a trapper, King George's men, Jesuit priests on the upper Columbia, or from Iroquois Indians in the Buffalo country, they cannot tell. They seemed to get it from all these sources about the same time. At all events, the more they heard, the more troubled became their hearts about the way they were to worship. They became more and more convinced that sun worship was not the right way. Many a yearly gathering or council was closed with, " If we could only find the trail of Lewis and Clark, and follow it up, we would come to the light or the truth about what we have heard."

They had heard that the white man had a book from God. That would tell them the right way to worship. At last, twenty-five years after Lewis and Clark had been among them, they " finished their

minds " or decided to seek for the trail and for the
Light.   Elder Billy Williams told me he well remembered the going out.   Billy was eight or ten years old
when they started, and rode out a piece of the way on
the pony behind his cousin, who was one of the four
who went.   Elder Billy often told me this wonderful
story.   The last time he did so, I translated it as he
told it, for the Rev. Dr. D. O. Ghormley, in July of
1894, a year before Billy died.

The four who went to St. Louis on that memorable
quest were :

1.   " Tip-ya-lah-na-jeh-nin " (Black or Speaking
Eagle); he died in St. Louis.   He was " Kip-ka-pel-i-
kan's " grandfather, or Pa-ka-lis.   I think he was one
of the chiefs who entertained Lewis and Clark in the
Kamiah Valley on their return trip, in 1806.   The
name is misspelled by them, " Tu-na-ach-e-moolt-olt."

2.   " Ka-ou-pu " (Man of the Morning or Daylight)
who was one of the two older ones.   His mother was
a Flathead, his father a Nez Perces.   He died in or
near St. Louis—perhaps at St. Charles.

3.   " Hi-youts-tohan " (Rabbit-Skin-Leggins) who
was of the White Bird band, part Palouse, but a Nez
Perces Indian.   He was Speaking Eagle's brother's
son.   (Yellow Bull is from the same band.)   He was
one of the two young men, and he alone lived to return.   He met the Nez Perces in great numbers in
the Buffalo country, Montana, told them all about his
visit and that the promise had been made to send a

man with the Book to them. He never came back among his people in the Nez Perces land. No one knows where he went. It is likely with the whites, for he loved them so well. That year about a hundred whites came in among them on the Buffalo ground.

4. " Ta-wis-sis-sim-nim" (No horns on his head, or little horns like an old buffalo), died on the road home—perhaps near the mouth of the Yellowstone. He was about twenty years old when he started. His two horses were brought back near to Lemhi. He was a doubter of their old beliefs.

There was a fifth one who started, a Flathead Indian, went a two days' journey and returned. Said he was too old to go on. So he is never talked of in connection with the company.

It seems quite natural that when the Nez Perces were perplexed about how and what to worship, their eyes and hearts should try to follow the trail of their trusted friends, believing if their troubles were laid before " the crowned ones," they would know the truth. Kip-ka-pel-i-kan, the grandson of Tip-e-lah-ne-yeh-nin, is at the present writing a member of the Second Church of Kamiah, and is over sixty years old.

This going out, Elder Billy well remembered, was in 1831 or 1832. Indians are not exact as to dates. Mrs. Eva Emery Dye, in " The Conquest" (p. 426), says it was 1831. This would be twenty-five years after Lewis and Clark had come among them in the

Kamiah Valley. Of course the older men, especially the chiefs, well remembered their white friends.

In gathering material for " The Conquest " (see p. 426), Mrs. Dye found this record in the Cathedral at St. Louis :

" Kee-pee-le-le, buried October 31, 1831, a ne Perce de la tribu des Chopooneek, nation appelée Tete Plate."

The name Kee-pee-le-le is doubtless meant for the family name, as it resembles the name of Speaking Eagle's grandson, Kipkapelikan. It was a very common thing in early days for a Nez Perces to have two, or even more names. Sometimes the people changed the name after some brave act or battle. More often the man had it changed himself, by making a present at some great gathering. If the " Aahs " were general, the people's consent was given. It was as he wished. He had a new name. The Christian Indian has no desire to change his name. It is but a few years ago that the wild ones tried to bring back the old custom. The agent brought this business to a sudden stop by announcing that they might lose their individual land by it—that they must keep the name written in their patents. So the name Tipyal-ahnahjeh-nin given here, and Keepeelele in the records of the St. Louis Cathedral, is no perplexity to me. He was a Nez Perces ; no question about that.

Their tradition is that the first time they heard the name Nez Perces applied to them, was in St. Louis

when the four who had been sent in search of the
light or truth about God, were sitting in silence in the
American Fur Company's rooms gazing at the many
who came curiously to see them and wondering where
they came from. At last one who was said to be
" wise " was brought in and he on short examination
said, they are the Nez Perces or Pierced Noses of the
lower Columbia. This misnomer has clung to them
ever since. Their own testimony is that they never
did pierce their noses.

It is strange that historians have made such careless
statements about this delegation—that they were Flatheads, or the Flathead branch of the Nez Perces.
There is no such branch. If they had been called
long-headed Nez Perces, instead of Flatheads, it would
have been more appropriate. I have never heard
that the Flatheads claimed the honour. Certain it is
that they never received much benefit from the delegation. The Flatheads are now a Roman Catholic
tribe. The Nez Perces here never dream that any
one doubts their statement. Of course, those brave
men had no idea of what results would follow their
mission, but back of this movement was the living,
loving Lord, who could see the end from the beginning, and as He looked westward down through coming
years could say, " I have much people there."

Those two younger men, when they had buried the
fathers who led them there, felt, no doubt, their mission
to be a sad failure. In their parting address in the

American Fur Company's rooms in St. Louis, one of them said, " I came to you over a trail of many moons from the setting sun. I came with one eye partly open for more light for my people who dwell in darkness. I made my way to you with strong arms, through many enemies and strange lands, that I might carry back much to them. I go back with both arms broken and empty. The two fathers who came with us, the braves of many winters and wars—we leave them here asleep by your great waters and wigwams. My people sent me to get the Book from heaven from the white men. You make my feet heavy with burdens of gifts, but the Book is not among them. When I tell my poor, blind people, after one more snow, that I did not get the Book—no word will be spoken. One by one they will arise and go out into silence. My people will die in darkness. No Book from the white man to make the road plain. " Kullo " (That is all).

One who had listened to this touching lament published it in the Pittsburg *Advocate*. The Methodists were stirred up to form a missionary society, or board, to meet this call. In 1834 Jason Lee, with his nephew, Daniel Lee, and laymen Sheperds and Edwards, were sent out to form a mission among the Indians, the Nez Perces. Under an escort furnished by Captain Wyeth they travelled. Wyeth stopped to establish Fort Hall. The missionaries pushed on to Fort Nez Perces, now Wallula, and from there, in company with Hudson Bay men, reached Vancouver, where Dr. McLoughlin was stationed. His kind treatment of these strangers—of any strangers, indeed—influenced the Methodists to start their mission in the Willamette Valley, instead of the Clearwater Valley.

In 1835 the American Board of Commissioners for Foreign Missions sent out the Rev. Samuel Parker, of Ithaca, N. Y., and Dr. Marcus Whitman, of Rushville, N. Y., to explore the Oregon country (this whole country from the Bitter Root to the sea was called Oregon then), with a view of forming missions among the Indians. At the Green River rendezvous on the Rocky Mountains they met many Nez Perces Indians, among them Ish-hol-hol-hoats-hoats (Lawyer)so named for his shrewdness by the Hudson Bay Company men, and Tuk-ken-sui-tas (Samuel). No doubt there they told of the search for the Book and the eagerness of the Nez Perces for a teacher who would show them the true way. It was there decided that Dr. Whitman should take two Nez Perces boys, Ites and Tueka-kas, or as Dr. Whitman called them, John and Richard, return to the East and ask for men and means to start a mission among the Nez Perces. The Indians promised to escort the Rev. Mr. Parker through the land. This promise they faithfully kept, taking him safely down to Fort Walla Walla, where he met P. C. Pambrum, chief clerk of the Hudson Bay Company.

This was in 1835. The Nez Perces knew that the " white head," Dr. McLoughlin, at Vancouver, had used his influence to send the missionaries which were sent by the Methodists to the Willamette Valley, instead of to the Clearwater Valley. Dr. Whitman, with his two Nez Perces boys, journeyed eastward from the Rocky Mountains in the company of the American Fur Company's men. The doctor made himself so companionable and useful, that his wants and the wants of the two Indian boys, were kindly met by the Fur Company's agents. They reached New York safely. The doctor reported to the American Board, who decided to establish a mission among the Nez Perces, as had been arranged with Whitman and Parker before leaving the Green River rendezvous in the Rocky Mountains.

February 20, 1836, as Mr. and Mrs. Spalding were wending their way over the crunching snow of Western New York, on their way as missionaries to the Seneca Indians, they were overtaken by Whitman, who wanted this good couple for mission work in Oregon. Questions and answers passed as they rode along. "It will take the summers of two years." "We can have the escort of the American Fur Company to the Divide, and there the Nez Perces will meet and guide the rest of the way." So the conversation went on until they reached the village of Howard, N. Y. Mrs. Spalding was left to decide the matter, which she did upon her knees, in an upper chamber in a tavern. "What about your health?" Mr. Spalding asked, when she returned her answer, "I will go.

REV. H. H. SPALDING

I like the command just as it stands," was her reply,
"' Go ye into all the world,' without any exceptions
for poor health." Mrs. Spalding was a weakly woman.
Intellectually and spiritually, she was fitted for this
undertaking. She had been sitting side by side with
her husband in the Greek and Latin classes in Lane
Theological Seminary in Cincinnati, when Beecher's
lectures were so much to that institution. Whitman
was soon afterwards married to Narcissa Prentis, of
Amity, N. Y. These were two grand young women
—although not alike in character. The Indians took
to Mrs. Spalding at once, giving as a reason, " She
had a quiet heart—was not excitable, and readily
picked up their language."

At Independence, Mo., they were joined by
Mr. W. H. Gray (afterwards Oregon's historian), who
had been appointed financial agent for the company.
He certainly had his hands full in caring for this company and its baggage, for they had with them material
for a blacksmith's shop, plows, seeds of all sorts, clothing to last two years, and wagon teams. At starting
they had three wagons, eight mules, sixteen cows, two
men, and those two Indian boys, who were indeed
helpful on the way. Little can we now conceive the
inconveniences, not to say hardships, of that journey.
There were rivers to ford, or skin rafts to be made for
crossing, mountains to ascend and descend where a
false step would mean broken bones or death.

Safely they reached the rendezvous in the Rocky

Mountains at Green River, in company with the Fur Company's men. Two days before they reached there they had a fright from the Indians, who, hearing of their approach, had come to meet them, but they soon saw a white cloth tied to a gun and knew they were friends. But how strange their actions ! Horses and riders alike seemed crazy with joy,—leaping, yelling, whirling round—no wonder the men, as well as the two women, were frightened. It *was* rather an unpleasant way the Nez Perces had to express their joy that the missionaries had indeed come.

They expected to meet Parker there according to agreement, but instead found a letter from him, carried there by Nez Perces hands.

The following is from Mrs. Spalding's diary:

July 4, 1836.   Crossed a ridge of land to-day called the Divide, which separates the waters which flow into the Atlantic from those which flow into the Pacific, and camped for the night on the head waters of the Colorado. The brave Nez Perces who have been awaiting our arrival at the rendezvous for several days, on hearing we were near, came out to meet us, and have camped with us to-night. They appear to be gratified to see us actually on our way to their country. Mr. Spalding, Dr. Whitman and Mr. Gray are to have a talk with the chiefs to-night.

July 6th. We arrived at the rendezvous this evening. Were met by a large party of Nez Perces, men, women, and children. The women were not satisfied short of saluting Mrs. Whitman and myself with a kiss. All appear happy to see us. If permitted to

reach their country and locate among them, may our
labours be blessed to their temporal and spiritual good.

July 18th. We have commenced our journey for
Fort Walla Walla, in company with Mr. Macleod.
The Nez Perces seem sadly disappointed because we
do not accompany them. They say they fear we will
not go with them. All appear very anxious that they
may be taught about God, and be instructed in the
habits of civilized life. One chief has concluded to
go with us, notwithstanding it will deprive him of the
privilege of securing a supply of meat for the winter.

The Indians you may be sure cast some keen looks
at the two white women. They presented the visitors with some fresh venison; also a piece of broiled
and roasted buffalo meat—roasted on a stick with more
sand than salt on it. In return for this compliment,
Ish-hol-hol-hoats-hoats (Lawyer) and Tak-en-sue-tis
(Samuel) were invited to supper with their white
friends. Lawyer would not have been the father of
his sons, if he had not tried to make a good impression upon the white friends there. Mrs. Lawyer was
with her husband on that trip, and took great delight
in telling me about it when she was a very old woman.
In the Nez Perces eyes, Mrs. Spalding was so kind, so
gentle, so altogether good. Mrs. Lawyer said, " Why,
she could talk quite well with us before we reached
our own land." [1]

The short letter from Dr. Parker said he had been

[1] Mrs. Spalding was a cousin of Dr. Ellinwood of the Foreign
Board.

treated kindly by the Indians, and showed that he was favourable to starting missions among the Nez Perces and the Cayuse. He went down to Vancouver, and from there visited the Methodist mission conducted by the Lees, uncle and nephew. Their mission was not strictly for Indians. There were many Canadians and half-bloods there, also whites. Mr. Parker returned home by way of the Sandwich Islands. Those Islands, which seem so far off to us now, were for some reason easily reached then. Perhaps because there was much travel by way of Cape Horn, and the Hudson Bay Company's furs were taken that way. Mr. Parker did a good work for the Church, which then knew so little about the needs of Oregon.

So the company went on its way to Fort Walla Walla. Other travellers had tried to take wagons with them. All but Whitman had to leave them at some point on the road. No roads, not even trails much of the way. At Fort Hall, Whitman was told it was simply impossible to take that wagon. He must give up and go the way like the rest. They did not yet know the man. He made a cart of two wheels, loaded the other two wheels and the swingle-tree upon it, and brought it through to Fort Boise, where he left it for a time until he could go back for it.

The Nez Perces kept close to their missionaries, from the Rocky Mountains to the Columbia, all following the Hudson Bay Company's traders. They reached Fort Walla Walla on the Columbia, Septem-

ber 2, 1836, a little more than four months after leaving the Missouri. According to their estimate they
had travelled 2,250 miles.

They were kindly received at the Fort by Mr. P. C.
Pambrum, Hudson Bay Company's agent at that point.
The tired ladies were helped from their horses, and
everything possible done for the comfort of all.
Cattle and horses were cared for as well. They rested
but a few days there. Then, in company of Pambrum, started off in boats for Vancouver. The hardships of the waterway equalled for a time the mountain roads—so many falls, so many portages to make
—but Vancouver was headquarters. All strangers felt
like paying their respects to the kind old " white
head " there, Dr. McLoughlin. Word had gone on of
the coming of the strangers, so he, with a friend,
stood at the landing, waving a welcome. Gallantly
offering his arm to Mrs. Whitman, he led her up the
beach to his home, followed by his friend with Mrs.
Spalding. They reached there September 12, 1836.

Everything that could be done was done for the
visitors in that then magnificent log house. It took
the ladies some time to understand domestic arrangements there, but when they did, they did the best they
could in a quiet way to improve conditions.

The subject discussed there was, where to locate.
Pambrum, from the upper country, constantly re-
minded the doctor of the claims of the Cayuse and
Nez Perces upon them.

So Messrs. Spalding, Whitman and Gray left the women in their comfortable quarters, and started up the river in search of locations. Mr. Gray was in favour of stopping at The Dalles, because the Indians delighted to gather at the salmon fisheries, but the Lord knew where He wanted them to pitch their tents. At Wallula they found their Nez Perces friends waiting for them, to guide them home. They were soon on their Cayuse ponies, with one for a packhorse. They went into camp where the Mill Creek falls into the Walla Walla, the Cayuse Indians slyly watching their movements. Can you not see the four ? Whitman, Spalding, Gray and Pambrum, around the camp-fire, discussing the advantages of that site for the mission ? For several days they explored the adjacent country, returning to the same camp at night. A stake was put down to mark the spot. This done, they returned, brought the tent, horses and mission goods, and began at once to put up a house, the Indians helping all they could in the work. This was the beginning of the mission house among the Cayuse Indians, at Wai-ye-lat-poo.

In a few days Whitman started with Mr. Spalding, Mr. Gray and the Nez Perces, up to the Clearwater country. On they travelled about one hundred and twenty miles, to the Clearwater River, selected a spot about two miles up the Lapwai Creek and twelve miles from what is now Lewiston. There they found good springs—always a matter of first importance with the

Indians. They knew just the best spot to lead their missionaries to. The place has lost none of its charms. Some of the old apple trees which Mr. Spalding planted are still there, and as the traveller now descends Thunder Hill and looks at the comfortable home of James Grant, a Nez Perces, he will say, if he knows the story, " No wonder that was the place chosen to pitch the buffalo tent in 1836." Soon after they had decided upon the locations, they returned to Waiyelatpoo where Dr. Whitman resumed work on his house on Mill Creek. Mr. Spalding went on to Vancouver and brought the ladies up. We can imagine Mrs. Whitman's fine voice leading in the praises about that altar, thanking God for all His kindness on the way. Mr. and Mrs. Spalding did not rest long there for it was now late in the fall. It was the 29th of November when Mrs. Spalding arrived at Lapwai. In a letter to her parents written soon after her arrival, Mrs. Spalding calls it " This dear spot." She says, " We are located among a people with whom we will be happy to spend our days."

At last, the Nez Perces had their long-expected missionaries.[1]

[1] See Gray's " Oregon," p. 109, where the statement is made that Rev. Samuel Parker and Dr. Whitman met the Nez Perces on the Rocky Mountains in 1835, where they had gone to meet the promised " man with the Book." Also p. 119, where in July, 1836, they again were waiting on the Rocky Mountain Divide for the expected teacher, and met Dr. Whitman there on his return from the East, with his wife and Mr. and Mrs. Spalding.

Only three weeks and three days did they have to live in the buffalo tent. By that time Mr. Spalding and Mr. Gray, with the help of the Indians, had built a log house forty-eight by eighteen feet. It took twelve Indians to carry one log from the river, three miles away. Eighteen feet of one end of that building was used by the family. The rest was a school room—Indian room—and a place of worship. Poor Mrs. Spalding! What a time she must have had to keep the people out of her end of the house at meal times. It was well she was a gentle, patient woman.

She soon had her school going. There was no trouble to get pupils near, for at that day the people were not living scattered in families, but in bands, in long houses or tents—something like the cattle, as one of their own people has said. If they felt so disposed, the whole community, or tribe, could easily pick up and pitch their tents near their teacher. Once the writing and reading were started, the progress would be fast, for ambition to excel each other is one of the leading traits of the Nez Perces character. The printing by hand of the lessons was very attractive to them, men, women and children. I have seen some of it which would be a credit to a present-day pupil. Mrs. Spalding could draw somewhat, and often made use of this art in her teaching of Bible truth. The Nez Perces believed in pictures. One of Miss S. L. McBeth's pupils, Enoch, said, in a dispute in her schoolroom, " It is so. I saw a picture of it." That settled the matter.

THE HOUSE BUILT BY MR. SPALDING IN 1837

This Picture Taken 1901

Mrs. Spalding not only taught books, but domestic arts as well. She taught her girls to knit and sew. If she taught them how to weave, they did not keep that up. Some of the old women whom I have known could read a little. Mr. Spalding helped in the school-room. All studied aloud, or followed the teacher in the pronunciation.

Mr. Spalding was a man of affairs—there was no agent then—no soldiers—no anything, or anybody, but the missionaries. Mr. Spalding was a faithful, earnest, strong man, but for all that, Mrs. Spalding had, and has, the warmest place in the people's hearts. Mr. Spalding tried hard to teach the people to cultivate the ground. He did much talking to them about how to do it. One day it was about the potato, while they were in the house at the foot of Thunder Hill. He explained how to plant and how to culti-vate it. Then he pared one potato—cut it in pieces, handing Billy a raw piece on the point of his pocket-knife. Billy tasted it and pronounced it "taats" (good). Billy's potatoes and garden the next year were the talk of the tribe, causing the young maiden who had rejected his suit the year before to reconsider the matter, and take him for her husband.

They had lived about a year in that beautiful spot at the springs, or as we now say, at the foot of Thun-der Hill. (Big Thunder, a chief, is buried on the top of the hill.) The "sent ones" as the Nez Perces called the missionaries, thought a better place for the mission would be on the banks of the Koos-koos-ki, or Clearwater River. So a more commodious log house was built there near the mouth of the Lapwai. The largest room was at first the schoolroom—the reception-room—the place for gatherings. A school-house was built later. This ground was, and is still, a favourite camping-place. There the long tent was pitched—perhaps 150 feet long, like the one Lewis and Clark saw in Kamiah, and there Mr. Spalding enclosed fifteen acres of ground to cultivate, not only for self-support, but for an object-lesson in agriculture. He felt he was as much a missionary when planting or hoeing his corn and potatoes, as when translating the book of Matthew into the native tongue. He was right. There he planted his orchard, and after seventy years have passed, the little gnarled apple trees stand. The gavel now used by the moderator of the Walla Walla Presbytery was made from a limb of one of these same trees, planted by Mr. Spalding's hands. The old house was torn down only a few years ago (in 1902), after serving for several years as a stable. The present owner of the land on which it was built, could not understand why the So-yap-po (whites) were coming, sighting around his stable so often—knocking off bits of stone from the old outside chimney, and going off as if they had found a precious thing. Many years before it became a stable, it was used by a deaf and dumb Indian. Mr. D—— went to the back room of his home one day. No answer to his

rap. He stepped in. Deafy was standing in front of
a small glass which hung upon the wall, his back to
the door, patiently pulling out every hair from his
chin with a small pair of tweezers. Now he saw why
the Nez Perces had no beards. A few of them now
have mustaches.

III

FIRST CHURCH IN OREGON TERRITORY

The Lapwai Mission—First Converts—First Mills—Printing Press—
Great Council at Lapwai—Dr. Elijah White—First Presbyterian
Church in Oregon Territory—The Spaldings Visit Weiyelatpoo—
Their Return to Lapwai—Arrival of New Missionaries—Additions
to Church at Weiyelatpoo.

THREE years had passed before the first two converts, Joseph (Tu-a-kas) and Timothy (Tam-mut-sin)
" finished their minds " to enter the new way. Four
or more years passed before any others confessed their
love for Christ. The school went on. At times nearly
two hundred in it, and then again but few. The
people, men and women, were anxious to learn,
spurred on to the work by their natural ambition to
excel each other. It matters little to them now if a
white person has a well-furnished house, but let one of
their own people advance in these things, that is
enough to make others move.

There at Lapwai a sawmill and grist-mill were built.
In this and in other work Mr. Spalding was ably assisted by Messrs. Gray and Rogers. Mr. Spalding had
more variety in his work at first than Mrs. Spalding
had. His preaching points were Alpowai, Sheme-
nekam (Lewiston) Lapwai, Askiwewa, Asotin and
Kamiah. He often went to visit their nearest white

48

neighbour, Dr. Whitman, one hundred and twenty miles away, leaving Mrs. Spalding with the people—then somewhere about three thousand. Only once did one of them say an insulting word to her, and he came near losing his life for it, so indignant were the people. Mrs. Spalding pleaded for him. The people have not yet forgotten it. On asking a few years ago who a certain woman was, the answer was, "She is the daughter of that man who insulted Mrs. Spalding." If Mrs. Spalding had not loved her work and felt His presence, what a burden her daily tasks of cooking, sewing and teaching would have been. No mail carrier to look for—and few books to read, one day was just like another.

What a red-letter day that must have been, in 1839, when a train of tired Cayuse ponies came over the Lapwai hills and stopped in front of the mission, bearing a present of a printing press from the native Church at Honolulu, Hawaiian Islands! Both missions, there and here, were under the American Board of Commissioners for Foreign Missions. Mr. E. O. Hall and wife came along with the printing press, to show how to use it. What a forward impulse was given to the schoolroom work, when a little elementary primer of twenty pages was passed around among the pupils! Of course they studied louder than ever, for old men and old women, as well as the children, were expected to commit to memory the lesson given them to print. Now here was the printing already done. Then came a little book, "Young Child's Catechism," just as we have it now, only it was printed in the Nez Perces language for them. What a prize! I find occasionally one of this early date, carefully rolled up—just ready to fall to pieces for very age.

After Dr. Elijah White's visit, the Code of Laws adopted for the government of the Nez Perces, was printed on this press and studied in school as a lesson. Mr. Spalding wrote at this time, " All they care for is the Bible and the Laws," meaning this code of Dr. White's. It is just the same now, the Bible is the book of books to them. Many hymns were translated and printed on the little press. They sing some of these old hymns yet. Mr. and Mrs. Spalding showed good judgment in the hymns they chose to translate; they were old hymns with the pith of the Gospel in them, such as " God loved the world of sinners lost" and " Come Holy Spirit." That little printing press did good work. When the mission was broken up, it reached Salem, Oregon, where the second newspaper of the Territory was published and called *The Oregon American Evangelical Unionist.* The press is now in the Historical Rooms at Portland, Oregon.

Dr. Elijah White, sub-agent for the United States, made a visit to the Nez Perces in 1842, at a great council at Lapwai at which twenty-two chiefs were present. At that council were Five Crows and Bloody Chief, the latter was ninety years old, and was

one of the speakers ; he had much to say about
Lewis and Clark. He really nominated Ellis for
chief, in an indirect way, by saying, " We sent three
of our sons to the Red River Settlement. Two of
them sleep with their fathers. One is here to-day.
I am tired and can say no more."

Dr. White told them that if the election of a head
chief were unanimous, they would meet the next
morning at ten o'clock, then dine together with the
chief on a fat ox at three P. M. There was much
talking to their white friends, Mr. McKinley and
Mr. Rogers, before they understood just what to do.
Ellis was elected. The feast was fully enjoyed, as
were the after-dinner songs, also. Then the pipe
passed around. I presume Mr. Spalding passed it—
without a puff himself—to the next one, for he taught
them to throw away tobacco with the bottles.

When all was over, Dr. White complimented the
Nez Perces for not once bothering him with begging
while on this visit. He said they were different from
all other tribes whom he knew. Then in the name
of his chief, the President of the United States, he
presented fifty hoes to Mr. Spalding and the chief, to
be given by them to the worthy poor.

The laws framed for the government of the Nez
Perces were then read and accepted.

Then the unit of value was the beaver skin. For
murder and the burning of a dwelling the offender
must die. For the breaking of any one of the other

nine laws, the punishment should be administered in lashes, the number of lashes to be decided by the chief. It is hard now to believe that the Nez Perces ever submitted to this.

The newly elected head chief, Ellis, had no easy time of it. The old people say that he taught them much about God—that they now see his teaching was right, but it ran so against their practices that they rejected it then. He became more and more unpopular with his people, and they got after him as I have known them to do since—like hornets from a disturbed nest, and stung him to death. He left them to follow their hearts, and took refuge over in the Buffalo country, Montana, where he died of smallpox, I think in 1846 or 1847. If it can be, they look back upon their treatment of their own Nez Perces chief, Ellis, with more shame than at the remembrance of Mr. and Mrs. Smith. Ellis's daughter, Mrs. Jehoshaphat, is living at this writing and is a member of the Meadow Creek congregation.

The first Presbyterian Church in Oregon Territory was organized August 18, 1838, by the missionaries of the American Board of Commissioners for Foreign Missions, at Weiyelatpoo, Dr. Whitman's station among the Cayuse Indians, or in other words, in Dr. Whitman's house. This was situated on the banks of the Walla Walla River near the mouth of Mill Creek. This point is distant from the new city of Walla Walla about seven miles.

The charter members were seven; Rev. Henry Harmon Spalding, a Presbyterian missionary from the Presbytery of Bath, N. Y.; Mrs. Eliza Spalding, his wife, also a missionary; Dr. Marcus Whitman, a Presbyterian elder, from Wheeler, Steuben County, N. Y., missionary; Mrs. Narcissa Whitman, his wife, a missionary; Joseph Maki; Mrs. Maria Kewua Maki, both natives of the Hawaiian Islands, who presented certificates from the church in Honolulu; Charles Compo, a French Canadian of mixed blood, who had been a Catholic.

Mr. Spalding was elected pastor of this church in the wilderness, and Dr. Whitman an elder. It was Resolved, " That this church be governed on the Congregational plan, but attached to the Bath Presbytery, of New York." The wonder is that the Nez Perces are not now either Methodists or Congregationalists, from the mixed state of things in early days.

A brave little company that was. Gathered from the ends of the earth to set up the banner of the Lord in such a lonely spot. The meeting was held in the home of Dr. Whitman—perhaps in Mrs. Whitman's schoolroom. It must have been full and the women with their little ones down on the floor, the mother every once in a while giving the baby board a shake to keep the little one from fretting, as it stood in its case so upright. Who else was there? I can find the record of only one white spectator, a Catholic, Pambrum, from Walla Walla, who charged Compo to think well before he left the mother church. Two years had nearly passed since Mr. Spalding, Dr. Whitman and their faithful wives began sowing Gospel seed in the fallow ground around them. Not one convert from either the Nez Perces or Cayuse tribes yet, to show that the Lord was blessing their work, but for all that, they did not doubt the promise, " My word shall not return unto Me void." He will fulfill all in His own time and way.

August 19, 1838, the day after the organization, the Lord's Supper was celebrated. The Master Himself was there. How their hearts burned within them, as He drew them closer to Himself than they ever had been before !

Those poor, ignorant Indians, men and women, who were watching every movement with intense curiosity. The bread and the wine ! What did that mean, and why was it not given to them as well? And then, the baptism of that little, eighteen-months' old John Compo—well, I know, every mother heart among them longed for the same to be done to her child, or children, if it would shield them in after life from harm. Of course, she thought it was some kind of a charm, connected with the Wy-ya-kin, or attending spirit.

What a strange-looking company filled that room ! Leggins, moccasins and the cover-all, blanket or skin of some animal; shells in their ears ; hatless, their heavy braids falling in front. So were the men. The women had their skin slips on, fringed with the same around the bottom. Few ornaments for them. The baby boards were covered with beads and shells and bangles. The consecrated leaders, or missionaries, had no eyes for these queer things, but were thinking of the time when the Spirit would plow up the soil and give life to the seed. We love to look back through the years—some of them dark, and trace the blessings which have come to this whole country from the doings of that day. And still there is more to follow!

What a visit that must have been to Mrs. Spalding, who had not seen the face of a white woman for nearly two years! How those two dear friends, Mrs. Whitman and Mrs. Spalding, who had travelled for months together, would talk as they worked—for sure I am, Mrs. Spalding did not sit with folded hands in that busy home at Waiyelatpoo. They strengthened each other's hearts by telling over God's care for them, and of His presence with them in their homes and in their work. Their discouragements were many, but back of them His promises.

The morning came when they must separate and the Spaldings return to Lapwai. The Cayuse ponies were brought up to the house, with their plaited horse-hair bridles tied under the jaws and the wooden saddles adjusted. The pack ponies were piled high with provisions and tents for the journey of one hundred and twenty miles. Many little packages of seeds and roots were in the bundles, to try in the Nez Perces country, so isolated that they only occasionally saw a trapper or trader, while the Whitmans saw about all the travel of the country, going by way of Walla Walla to the headquarters at Vancouver. Mrs. Whitman would have her little presents packed in, too. Little Eliza was in her mother's arms, watching all the preparations for starting.   These two white women talked of the expected missionaries. Mrs. Gray was looked for any time now, with her husband, at the Nez Perces mission, and Mrs. Whitman would have others with her, for a time at least.   So they stood talking, while the men made all secure on the ponies. They planned a visit to the Clearwater home. God kindly veils our eyes, so that we can only see a few steps before us at most. All was ready.   It would be very like Mrs. Spalding to say, " Come, let us go into the house and spend a few minutes in prayer together before we separate." Then there would be another meeting of the newly formed church, for of course the French Canadian, Compo, with his Nez Perces wife, and the Hawaiian Islander, with his wife, mission workers, were all there to see the friends start off.   There, on their knees, in that now sacred spot, they consecrated themselves anew to the Master, asking blessings upon each other " while we are absent one from another," and if the hymn sung was not " God Be With You Till We Meet Again," that was the song of the heart.

How much Mr. and Mrs. Spalding had to talk
about—as they rode along meeting at times the smiling faces of their own Nez Perces on their way going to hunt on the Blue Mountains. They were tired
of the heat and the dust of the Lapwai Valley, and
their bit of corn and garden stuff was stored in the
" we-kash." So they had light hearts on their journey. It was indeed a pleasant road, or trail—for the
four or six-horse teams, with a trail wagon behind,
had not yet cut up the road, as they have now, com-
pelling the traveller to follow his way through a cloud
of dust. The fording-places were not dangerous.
The rivers were low. As they compared the two
tribes of Cayuse and Nez Perces, they would say,
" Our lines have fallen to us in pleasant places; we
have a goodly heritage."

On they went—to find a deserted village! For if
the Nez Perces had not gone one way, they had another. Most of them over the Bitter Root Mountains into the Buffalo country. " Might be back when
the snow flew. Might not be back for year." Fine
travellers, the Nez Perces were then. Anywhere was
home, where they could pitch a tent or find enough
fish, game and roots to live upon. In those days it
was a feast or a famine—eat, while they had anything to eat, then for days without anything. The
eating three times a day came in afterwards, as a part
of the teaching of the Gospel. When they had meat,
they ate meat. They do not object to a variety, now.

Mr. and Mrs. Spalding had plenty to do to provide for the coming winter, with its incoming missionaries. Mr. Gray and his young wife were expected soon. There were no regular mails, and so many hindrances to be met in the way of travelling then. But before a full month had passed after the organization at Waiyelat-poo the names of nine new missionaries were added to the roll of the new church. This was September 2, 1838.

These were William Gray, who had been with Mr. Spalding at the Clearwater mission, arrived with his wife. They were Presbyterians, also Mr. Cornelius Rogers. These were commissioned as helpers in the Nez Perces mission ; Rev. A. B. Smith and wife, for the Nez Perces mission, Congregationalists ; Rev. Elkanah Walker, with his wife, Mary, Congregationalists ; Rev. Cushing Eells, with his wife, Myra, Congregationalists. Revs. Walker and Eells, with their wives, did not re-main long at Waiyelatpoo. They opened a mission station among the Spokanes, in the spring of 1839, at Thsi-na-kain, six miles north of the Spokane River, and faithfully planted the Gospel seed for nine years. Yet was there not a convert to Christianity ; the seed was only buried—not lost. The quickening time came, to the Spokanes as to the Nez Perces, long after the missionaries had left them.

Mr. Gray, afterwards Oregon's historian, and Mr. Rogers, put new life into the mission on the banks of the Clearwater. Fifty years afterwards, at the Semi-

Centennial in the Lapwai Church, the old people had much to tell of the doings of those days. Some of the old women claimed to have helped to build the mill. I do not doubt it. They would be more efficient workers than the men, for the men considered hunting and fishing their part of the family work. Well did the old people remember Mr. Gray and Mr. Rogers and the grist-mill. An improvement indeed the grist-mill was, the women thought, over the old stone mortar in which they pounded the kouse, to make flour for bread. To the poor women, it had been pound, pound, never ending, a monotonous sound, which Lewis and Clark said, while in the Kamiah Valley, reminded them of a nail factory. The wisdom of the " So-yap-po " was all the talk. One of the old millstones lay for years near the grinding place at Lapwai. Then Henry Spalding, Mr. Spalding's son, took it away, intending to place it in the Idaho exhibit at the Chicago World's Fair. And in 1897 Ex-Governor McConnell had it removed to the University of Idaho, at Moscow, Idaho, where it still remains.[1]

Rev. A. B. Smith and wife remained for a time at Waiyelatpoo. In 1839 they opened a mission station in the beautiful Kamiah Valley, sixty miles beyond

---

[1] The stones for the grist-mill were of granite, about three feet in diameter and one foot thick. These were obtained in the vicinity of Peck, Idaho, and floated down about forty miles on a raft to the mouth of the Lapwai.

Lapwai, an isolated place, indeed. Ellis was chief at Kamiah at this time. Ellis was one of several Indian boys who had been sent by the Hudson Bay Company to the Red River Settlement, Canada. There were five boys, Ta-wa-to-wa, a Cayuse, Thomas Geary's father, of the Spokanes. I do not know who the others were—or if they were Nez Perces, two soon after died. Ellis was said to be overbearing and this was not surprising, with his limited education, among his ignorant people. He was much honoured by the whites. Lawyer was there at that time, a young, ambitious man. When Mr. Smith talked to the people in the fall of '39, they told him he might put up a house, but he must not enclose or plow any land. A jealousy between Lawyer and Ellis, a strained relationship between Mr. Spalding and some of the missionaries, made an unhappy winter for these lonely missionaries in Kamiah, the Indians often crowding in upon them demanding food. Mrs. Smith was a delicate woman, whom the Indians called "the weeping one." No doubt she had cause for tears.

When the spring came, Mr. Smith began plowing a piece of ground, with James Hines, now our oldest minister, riding one of the unwise ponies to guide the plow. At once the people appeared upon the ground, forbade another furrow to be turned, and told Mr. Smith to "Go! Go!" He told them he would as soon as he could find a way to go. He made a large canoe and came down the swollen river so dangerous at that time of the year, an Indian would hesitate to try the journey. But very glad they were to get down and out. They went to the Whitman mission and spent a time there; then to the Hawaiian Islands and at length reached their own eastern home.

The mission in the Kamiah Valley then, so far as we can see, was a failure. The Lord may look upon it differently.   Mr. Smith must have been a man of a good spirit, for more than twenty years afterwards he wrote, inquiring in the kindest way after some of the leaders of that trouble.   With heads bowed, and shame-covered faces, they heard of his inquiries.

It is not hard for me to see the three children of Mr. and Mrs. Spalding playing about the old home. Eliza may have carried little baby on her back, tied on there in her mother's shawl, while Martha Jane trotted along at her side, with her Indian doll in a te-kash (baby board), which she passed over her head, the strap fixed so that the te-kash was high up on her back or shoulders. The playing mother of the little girls in the long house near the mission house was just as fashionable then as it is to-day.   Other customs may change, but with heathen or Christian, the love for the children remains, strong and tender.   Henry Hart, Mr. Spalding's boy, no doubt practiced shooting at a mark, with his flint arrow-heads, failing to shoot a bird upon the wing as his little red friends could easily do; then he would turn his attention to the magpies, of which there were plenty stepping around.

Then all together, they would trip down to the shore and in the deep, white sand, hunt arrow-heads. The river, with the beautiful stones so clearly seen at the bottom, was by the Indian children no more to be dreaded than the land. No doubt, after the drowning of the only child of Dr. Whitman, the little Spaldings had many charges about the danger of going into the streams. They would look with great admiration at the wise Nez Perces children as they capered about in the water, diving and swimming across the river, the skin dress rolled up and carried over on the head of the swimmer. Or if they jumped in, moccasins and all, what did that matter? They obeyed the impulse. Mother would neither whip nor scold. She would only say, " Es-ta-es-ta wa-tu-taats " (My child, that is not good), and patiently scrape more skins for clothes and shoes. Oh! the happy, unfettered childhood of Indian life! But in after years, the selfish, willful-tempered ways of men and women show the results of such training, or want of training.

Mr. Spalding's body now rests under a clump of locust trees near to where the long house stood, and to the play-ground of the children—rests, until he, with his spiritual children, together rise, to meet their glorified Lord.

The first Mrs. Spalding is buried in the Willamette Valley. For eleven years Mr. and Mrs. Spalding had worked patiently, with little in those years to encourage them.

We have already spoken about the organization of
the First Church of Oregon at Waiyelatpoo, August
18, 1838, with seven charter members, all whites perhaps with the exception of Compo, a half-blood French
Canadian. Also that in September of the same year,
the number was increased by nine new members, making in all, sixteen. Somewhere near this time the
name of James Conner, a white, appears upon the roll.
These nine persons were all missionaries, or helpers in
the missions. During the time from the organization
in 1838 to the breaking up of the missions in 1847, we
find the names of a few more whites enrolled. Let us
now look at the rank and file, or lay members of the
church, the Indians :

Joseph (Tu-eka-kas), a Nez Perces Indian ; Timothy
(Ta-moot-sin), also a Nez Perces ; these were the first
Nez Perces to confess their faith in Christ, just three
years after Mr. and Mrs. Spalding came among them.
Joseph turned back to Egypt, but Timothy was faithful, not only to God, but to his white friends. A
short time after the Yakima war, when Colonel Steptoe, still over in the Palouse country, found himself
entrapped, the natives on the outside dancing and
having a good time over it, it was Timothy who with
his brothers knew the ground and that there was an
unguarded place in the rocks, and he quietly guided
Steptoe and his band through it and went with him
ninety miles to a place of safety among his own
people who cared for the wounded and crossed the

troops over the dangerous river. Timothy's kind old face comes now before me, as I saw it last, in 1881.

May 14, 1843, on profession of their faith, the following Indians were received by the advice of Mr. Littlejohn. Some of them had been examined three years and others eighteen months before:

Lyman, originally a Snake Indian, had been taken a slave in war; Lois, his wife, received at the same time; Levi, brother of Timothy; Luke; Eunice, wife of Luke; Hesekiah, Cayuse chief; Asenath, wife of Joseph; Fannie, wife of Timothy; Olive, wife of Oliver.

And June 24, 1843, the following natives were added on profession of their faith in Christ: John Casut, from the Catholics; Ruth, a very old woman; Lot; David; David's wife, Rhoda; Jude; Jude's wife, Mathilda; Titus; Levi; Bartholomew; which added to the eleven Indians on the roll makes twenty-two natives. Mr. Spalding and his elder, Dr. Whitman, spent three days examining these last applicants for membership. Delia's name was added, May, 1846.

Before the breaking up of the church or mission, a number of whites had withdrawn from the mission and left for other points, taking their certificates from this church, leaving the Indians as the body of the church.

During the first years Mr. Spalding spent among the Nez Perces, he had made no elders and organized no churches among them. He had what he called " ordained deacons," as helpers.

To look at these few Indian names on the roll of
the first church, it seems but a scant return for the
eleven years of patient seed-sowing of these early missionaries. But in 1855 an investigation was made of
results, showing that in three lodges numbering forty-
five persons, among the Cayuse, and in the homes of
about one-third of the Nez Perces (one thousand persons), regular morning and evening worship, and public worship, was kept up, with singing of the Nez
Perces hymns and reading of the book of Matthew,
which Mr. Spalding had translated for them eight
years before. No, no, the seed had not been lost, but
buried deep under the old customs and the influence
of the white man's vices, before the quickening came.

Mr. Spalding married a second time while in the
Willamette Valley. Although his home was there,
his heart was among the Nez Perces. In his absence,
public worship was conducted among the Nez Perces
by a few of the leading men. They held tenaciously
to the forms of worship he had taught them.

He returned to the Nez Perces land in the fall of
1862 under government appointment, as Superintendent of Education. This office was abolished in
1865. During those three years Mr. Spalding was
with them, he led them in spiritual things. One of his
preaching points was where the town of Lewiston
now stands.

IV

THE WHITMAN MASSACRE—THE SPALDINGS LEAVE LAPWAI

Dr. Whitman—His Journey East—He Returns with a Company of Emigrants—Finds Unfavourable Conditions at Weiyelatpoo—Whitman Massacre—The Nez Perces Restless—Mr. and Mrs. Spalding Leave the Work Among Them.

SIX busy, prosperous years had passed since Dr. Whitman and his efficient wife had started the mission among the Cayuse Indians at Weiyelatpoo. In September, 1842, he was called as a physician to Fort Walla Walla, and while there a number of the Hudson Bay Company's boats arrived, bringing several traders and Jesuit priests for the Interior.

Just while this company was seated at the dinner table the overland express from Canada came in, bringing the news that a company of emigrants from the Red River settlement in Canada were already at Colville. So great was the excitement and joy at the news that a young Catholic at the table sang out "Hurrah for Oregon, the Americans are too late, the country is ours."

Dr. Whitman sat there with both ears open listening to comments which confirmed his suspicion that there was a well-matured plan to bring on these British subjects to hold the country while Governor Simpson would go on to Washington to settle the question of boundaries, on the plea that there were already numerous and permanent settlements made, and that this work would be done so quickly that no information could reach Washington in time to prevent it.

The Doctor " finished his mind" right then and there, that he would make an effort to thwart this plan and in two hours after he sat in old Fort Walla Walla listening to the exuberant expressions, he reached Weiyelatpoo. His look and manner as he entered his home, showed that his mind was filled with a great purpose. He was not long in announcing his plan to save Oregon for God and his country. A. L. Lovejoy, who had but a few days before reached the Whitman station with some emigrants, agreed to go back with the Doctor and in twenty four hours they were on their way to the States, leaving Mrs. Whitman, the faithful wife, to " tarry by the stuff."

Then came that ride, that wonderful ride for five months, and the hardships which can never be fully described. He started October 3, 1842, at the beginning of winter, to cross mountains and rivers and much of the way without trail or guide. At Fort Hall they found that emigrants on their way to Oregon had been turned in another direction, because they were told that the road from there to the Columbia was impassable. All this talk was a part of the political plan to keep American citizens from reaching the fair land of Oregon.

At Fort Hall a less courageous man than Whitman, would certainly have turned back. He was facing two great obstacles, hostile tribes to meet, and crossing the Rocky Mountains in the dead of winter. He considered this and decided, although it would add one thousand miles to his journey, to swing around by the Santa Fé trail, and even this road was a perilous one.

At one time they were snowed up in a deep canyon for four days and in attempting to get out were lost in a blinding snow-storm and wandered about all day. Finally the guide saw the ears of his mule bent forward, and said as he jumped on his back and gave him a loose rein, " he will guide us." The others did the same and soon found themselves back to the camp they had left in the morning, where there was wood to put upon the still live coals. Look at this resourceful man near the head waters of the Arkansas. There they found that all the wood was on the other side of the river, with the ice too thin to walk upon. Dr. Whitman taking an ax in one hand and a willow stick in the other, lay breast down upon the ice and worked himself across, cut the wood, and returned in the same way, pushing the wood before him.

He reached Washington in March and found Secretary Webster and President Tyler hard to convince of the feasibility of taking emigrants with wagons through to the Columbia. Governor Simpson had made this appear impracticable. So worthless did

Oregon appear to be at headquarters that the United
States was on the point of trading it off for a cod
fishery on the coast of Newfoundland. Dr. Whitman's strong, persistent arguments, led the President
to promise, that if Dr. Whitman would establish a
wagon route through the mountains to the Columbia,
he would use his influence to hold Oregon until they
could hear whether or not the expedition was success-
ful. Then as the Doctor travelled along on his return
with the emigrants, we see the tenderness of the man
as he cared for the sick, cheered the discouraged and
inspired all by his own bravery. He would be out
in advance hunting the best road, or the safest ford
at the rivers. See him guiding and directing in
crossing the dangerous quicksand at the Grande River.
Fearing the loss of some of the teams, all were tied
together, while the Doctor forgetting self rode here,
there and everywhere strengthening weak hearts.
At length on September 5, 1843, the last emigrant
wagon emerged from the shade of the Blue Mountains
upon the banks of the Columbia. In looking back
upon this all round missionary as he strengthened the
stakes and lengthened the cords of the Master's kingdom, we must say he was surely raised up of the Lord
for the work he accomplished.

At Waiyelatpoo

Dr. Whitman spent one year in the East on
his journey on business both for the Church and

government, and returned to Waiyelatpoo in October, 1843, bringing eight hundred and seventy-five settlers for Oregon. Their one hundred and eleven wagons, two thousand cattle and horses, and equipments made an imposing train to the eyes of the Indians. The Doctor on his return found things in a bad condition. The grist-mill was burned, and all about the mission premises neglected. Mrs. Whitman, because of unkind treatment from the Indians, had taken refuge at the Methodist mission in The Dalles. The Doctor found many of the Indians sullen, and " with a different face" towards him. They had doubtless heard much at the Hudson Bay traders' post near them, Fort Walla Walla, as to the object of his visit to the East.

Furthermore, the Indians are shrewd readers of faces, and they understood pretty well what was going on, for the King George's men were just as anxious to take Oregon for their king as Whitman was to have " the Boston men " take it for America. It all meant to the poor, suspicious natives, nothing more nor less than, " The whites are going to take away our land, and make us slaves." They had councils and councils, but what could they do?

As the years passed on, more and more emigrants came. All who stopped at the Whitman mission were kindly treated and helped on to their destination. Other influences were at work, that all together, caused the brave hearts at Waiyelatpoo to sink within them. Not only the Whitman station was troubled, but all the missions—especially the Nez Perces. The people had "different faces" there. There was then, and still is, much intercourse between the two tribes. The school on the Clearwater was not so well attended. Many of the Nez Perces got " tired of working like women." They became insolent to Mr. Spalding. Mr. Spalding and Dr. Whitman met, and talked and prayed over these things as often as they could, but they were one hundred and twenty miles apart, and could not trust letters to go between them often.

Mr. and Mrs. Gray and Mr. Rogers had left the Nez Perces mission. The Kamiah station was deserted. Mr. Spalding had, at different times, helpers in his school, for since Eliza, Henry Hart and Martha Jane had come to the Spalding home, Mrs. Spalding could not teach as in her first years. But through all these anxious days they could see the Spirit had not left the mission, for here and there, He was touching hearts.

But the clouds grew darker and darker. Many were sick and dying among the Cayuse. Measles had been brought in by the emigrants, and this disease, with them, as with all natives, often proved fatal. The treacherous Joe Lewis, a French, half-blood Catholic, employed at the Whitman station, told that he had overheard the plot talked over between Mr. Spalding and Dr. Whitman, to kill the natives and take their land, that Whitman had advised quick work, but

that Mr. Spalding said, " No, do it gradually." Joe
Lewis was assisted in stirring up hatred by Joe Stan-
field, a Frenchman.   Dr. Whitman and thirteen others
were massacred by the Cayuse Indians, November 29,
1847.   Doubtless these sainted ones now know why
the Lord permitted such fearful work to go on.

Mr. Spalding knew something of the sickness and
of the many deaths from disease at Waiyelatpoo and
must go and comfort and help his friend.   He had
reached the Umatilla, about forty miles from Waiyelatpoo, at the time of the massacre.   Not knowing of
it he went on until he was within three or four miles
of the station, at which point he met a Catholic priest
who told him about it.   He turned his pony's head
homeward, and fled for his life, for it was a part of the
plan to destroy the Nez Perces mission, also.   Mr.
Spalding's horse got away from him, so he was compelled to walk the most of the way, travelling at night
and hiding through the day.   Barefooted and almost
exhausted he reached home on the seventh day.

While he was away, a Mr. Canfield, who had fled
from Waiyelatpoo, came to Mrs. Spalding and told
her all about the massacre, but advised her not to
mention it to the Nez Perces.   She understood the
Indian heart better than he did—trusted her Christian
Indians, and told them all about it.   They all thought
Mr. Spalding was killed also.

It was Sabbath morning that she stood in her door,
talking with Jacob, Eagle, and some others.   They

advised her to flee with them to their camp, where they could take better care of her and the children. Her answer was, " I will not flee on the Sabbath day. The Lord can take care of me here." They had a little council around the corner of the house. Then returned to her to say, " If you will keep the Sabbath, we will keep you."

This is the last picture we have of this brave woman, as she stood framed in that cabin door, and no wonder the Nez Perces have been a Sabbath-keeping people, with such an example as this before them. She left her home on Monday morning. It was pillaged by wild Nez Perces. She doubtless would have shared Mrs. Whitman's fate if she had been found alone.

Mr. Spalding got back in a worn-out condition, but happy to find his family alive. He did not know whether his little girl, Eliza, was living or not. She was in the Whitman home at the time of the massacre. She was not killed, however.

Soon after this, the Cayuse War began. All the Indian missions in this region were then broken up. Mr. Spalding, wife and family, were guarded to Fort Walla Walla, now Wallula, by forty Nez Perces. They passed on down, and settled in the Willamette Valley, where Mrs. Spalding died in 1851. Hers is a most honoured name among the Nez Perces to-day.

After the Cayuse War, all that were left of the once powerful Cayuse were, with the Walla Wallas, put on the Umatilla Reservation, where they have lost their language. The Nez Perces is the language spoken on that reservation. Many Cayuse have intermarried with the Nez Perces, but there is no boasting here of their blood. They have heard too often, " That is the tribe that killed Whitman." They rejected the message, killed the messenger, and have lost their identity as a tribe.

V

THE GREAT REVIVAL

Indian Treaties—Chief Joseph, White Bird and Looking Glass Refuse
to Give Up their Land—Agency Established—July Camp for Racing, Drinking and Gambling—Coming of the Yakima Ministers—
The Great Revival—Mr. Spalding's Return—His Death.

FROM the time Mr. Spalding left the mission, in
1847, until his return as a missionary in 1871, twenty-
four years after, little had been done for the spiritual
improvement of the Indians. During that time
treaties had been made. The first, in 1855, was made
with Governor Stevens acting for the government.
In this treaty, the Nez Perces were to give up the land
they claimed from the Blue to the Bitter Root Mountains, and go within the prescribed reservation, " where
they would never again be disturbed while the sun
shone or the water ran." This treaty was ratified
in 1859. The next year the gold mines of Oro Fino
were discovered on the reserve, and the gold mines of
Florence and other places in Western Idaho, and men
in countless numbers rushed across the reserve, to
reach the gold.

A new treaty was made in 1861 which was never
ratified. But that did not matter. The town of
Lewiston, on the desired strip, was laid out, and be-

came the first capital of Idaho—on the Nez Perces Reservation!

In 1863 another treaty was made, which was ratified in 1867, in which that part of the reserve lying north of the Snake and Clearwater Rivers and South Fork of the Clearwater, was given up. There was much opposition to this and the tribe was divided into treaty and non-treaty men. Chief Joseph, White Bird and Looking Glass refused to give up their beloved valleys. The Wallowa Valley, especially dear to Joseph, in heart he still felt it was his. This was the main cause of the Joseph war. Lawyer and about fifty of the leading men signed the treaty, and for this he was looked upon as untrue to his people.

Changes came in with these treaties. The agency was established at the mouth of the Lapwai, and the Fort four miles up Lapwai Creek, and from the soldiers especially demoralizing influences went out. This, with the old, dirty heathenism, brought the Nez Perces low indeed. But through it all, they kept a form of worship, losing, however, in this period, all but the three great commandments, " Remember the Sabbath day to keep it holy," " Thou shalt not kill," and " Thou shalt not steal." Things, not hearts, were meant by the word " steal " to them. A woman who would not, even when hungry, steal a piece of bread, would think it nothing more than fun to steal a man, or husband, from another woman. There was no word in the Nez Perces language for " husband."

Lying was nothing to be ashamed of. The only shame was in not being smart enough to conceal it or in being found out. According to their ideas, there was no sin in telling a lie the first time. There was a little sin if told the second time, but the third time, it was unpardonable. Any one understanding this, and putting the question three times, would be sure to get the truth the third time. This is some of the old teaching of their heathenism.

Drinking and fighting were common. The white men's methods of gambling were added to their own old ways. Gambling was always a favourite pastime with them. Such a mix-up of heathenism, white men's vices, and religion was perhaps never known before. And how they all did enjoy it! Especially at their great annual July camp for drinking, racing and "swapping wives," up in the beautiful Kamiah Valley. Billy often told me, "Me always had seven gallons of whiskey then."

The camp was there, because it was near their best kamas ground, the Weippe, and it was at that season, July, because the se-with, the kamas, and the kouse could then be found. Not only the Nez Perces would gather there, but strangers from neighbouring tribes would come hunting these roots.

Now, right into such a wild, degraded camp as this, in June 1870, came four young Yakimas, from Father Wilbur's Methodist mission on the Yakima reserve. The leader was George Waters. They began preaching to the Nez Perces. The spirit was so manifestly present that the camp became a " Bochim," and is still called " The Place of Weeping." This was near the ground upon which Lewis and Clark camped in the spring of 1806. It is not far from where the depot of the Northern Pacific Railway Company now stands.

At the time of this spiritual awakening, there was no Mr. Spalding there, and no white missionary. Just God and their guilty souls. Then and there, they threw away their bottles, their pipes, the feathers and tails of animals, and their wives. The wives were not easily thrown away. The men had many councils and much discussion as to which one to retain, and whom to cast away. They could have said, as did the Jews in the time of Ezra, " Neither is this the work of one day, or two, for we are many who have transgressed in this thing."

During that great revival meeting at Kamiah, a great many couples stood up and were married by one ceremony. In after years some of them were troubled about the strength of the bond in their case. Felix, years afterwards, took his matronly wife up to Robert, the native minister at Kamiah, and was married—" for sure."

The feathers and tails which were thrown away were emblems of their attending spirit, the " Wy-ya-kin," and when these were discarded, it was confessing, " I trust in you no longer."

Many at this camp took hold of the promises and became truly sons of God, and now, after more than twenty-eight years, I can sit in any one of our six churches among the Nez Perces, look around upon the old people, and say this or that man or woman was spiritually born there in that camp.

Was there such great power in these Yakimas? Were they so gifted? Ah! no. Acquaintance with the leading one in after years convinced me that the Lord had used a very feeble instrument to accomplish a great work.

The leader, George Waters, married into the Nez Perces Timothy family, and came back to Lapwai and Kamiah often to preach to the people. Too often! So thought the good Presbyterian agent, John Monteith, who explained to him that when the government parcelled out the reservations, the Nez Perces were given to the Presbyterian Church to care for. Waters decided to do as Langford did about his claim, " Bide his time," or, in other words, wait until the reservation would be opened. Then any denomination would have the right to come in. He had to wait about twenty years, but then, in he came, clothed with the authority of his Conference to open a Methodist mission among the Nez Perces.

We acknowledge to some anxiety on this subject, fearing division in our churches, for his name had been a household word for many years. Jonah, who had been a member of the Presbyterian Church, with his family had left us some time before, to rally around the Methodist banner. He now became one of George Waters's followers. A church was built at the mouth of the Sweetwater Creek on Jonah's farm.

The Yakima minister, George Waters, was a kind, gentle man. He mingled freely with our church people, but did not add to his own denomination. He became discouraged, and after a few years spent among the Nez Perces he returned to his own people. The little church on Jonah's farm was soon afterwards locked up. It is locked still.

That great awakening in the Kamiah camp only showed that in the Lord's own time and way He fulfills His promise, " My word shall not return unto Me void." It was only a quickening of seed planted in the early days of the mission. The work begun on that Kamiah camp ground extended through years.

In 1871, Mr. Spalding was sent back by the Presbyterian Board of Foreign Missions to gather in the sheaves. At the same time, Rev. H. T. Cowley was sent as teacher to Kamiah. He was a Congregationalist. He was a great help to Mr. Spalding in those busy years, and the people still have a " good remembrance " of him.

About this time the government built two churches for the people, one in Kamiah and the other in Lapwai. Mr. Spalding found conditions had changed since he spent his first eleven years among the Nez Perces. Then, he was their missionary, teacher, agent—their all in all. Now, the agent, Mr. John Monteith, a capable man, expected Mr. Spalding to keep to his own department, the spiritual affairs. But the people would come to Mr. Spalding with all their troubles for his advice, and from this grew strained relations between the agent and missionary. So the Presbytery which met at Lapwai in the spring of 1873 advised Mr. Spalding to make his home in Kamiah. He felt as badly about moving from Lapwai to Kamiah as a later missionary did to move from Kamiah to Lapwai.

He went up to Kamiah and began teaching a class of men for church work, whom he used as helpers in his missionary work among their own and neighbouring tribes. Old as Mr. Spalding was now—nearly seventy—he was much of the time in the saddle. His preaching stations among the Nez Perces were still Alpowai, "She-me-ne-kam (Lewiston, Lapwai, Asotin, North Fork, and Kamiah). He went with his helpers, among the Spokanes, where Revs. Eells and Walker had been, and often among the Umatillas and once among the Yakimas. It seemed to be one continual revival among the Nez Perces for years. He baptized hundreds of adults as well as children. His own statement, made in November, 1873, was :

" Received into the Lapwai church 155 males, and 189 females. Into Kamiah, 123 males and 188 females. Spokane, 112 males and 141 females. Whole number of adults, Lapwai, 344 ; Kamiah, 311 ; Spokane, 253. Whole number received into the First Church of

Oregon since 1836, 961." In thought at least, he still looked upon all as belonging to the First Church of Oregon, which, as we have seen, was organized at Waiyelatpoo.

In the fall of 1873, Miss S. L. McBeth arrived at Lapwai as teacher in the government school. In those days the Presbyterian Board had the privilege of nominating teachers for all government schools on Presbyterian reserves. Her time overlapped Mr. Spalding's by about one year. Mr. Spalding sickened in Kamiah, and was brought down to Lapwai, where he died among his people, August 3, 1874. He is buried not far from the Lapwai church, in a locust grove, near to his old mission house which was built in 1837, "aged seventy years, eight months, and seven days." " Blessed with many souls as seals to his ministry." He was a peculiar, faithful, strong man.

After Mr. Spalding's death in 1874, until the coming of Mr. Deffenbaugh, in 1878, the two pulpits of Kamiah and Lapwai were supplied a part of the time by white ministers connected with the government schools, as follows : Rev. George Ainslie, 1872–1875 ; Rev. S. N. D. Martin, 1875–1879 ; Rev. Warren Norton, 1875–1876; Rev. R. N. Fee, 1876–1878 ; also W. J. Monteith, J. R. Thompson and Prof. J. M. Conyer.

All vacanies were supplied by the native pupils of Miss S. L. McBeth's class, she directing their work.

Rev. Wm. Monteith, father of the agent, whose

home was with his son at Lapwai at the agency, preached for a time in the Lapwai church.

Mr. Spalding had ordained three deacons—virtually elders—in the Kamiah church, before he died. These were, Lawyer, Solomon Whitman, Jonathan Williams, known as Billy Williams.

No elders were ordained in Lapwai until 1876, when the elders ordained were, Levi, Timothy, Lot, Jude.

Lapwai, from the earliest time, had been considered an important preaching place. Not long ago I found one of our good Lapwai elders, Abraham Brooks, lying apparently asleep under a shade tree. When I spoke, he rose up, saying, " I have just been thinking over the past." He lived much of his time in the past after he lost his sight. He said, " I can see. Mr. Spalding did much hard work here, but the churches were not set in order until after Miss S. L. McBeth came."

VI

MISS S. L. McBETH

Leaves From Her Diary—Her School and First Pupils—Translates Nez Perces Hymns—Visit From Gen. O. O. Howard—Trouble From Chief Joseph's Band Compels Her to Leave Kamiah—Nez Perces Guard to Lapwai.

Miss S. L. McBeth's consecrated life among the Nez Perces can best be understood by looking over a few leaves from her diary. It will be seen that she believed she had a special call to work among Indians.

FAIRFIELD, IOWA,
September 5, 1858.

The duties of the day were over, the last class dismissed, the bright intelligent faces and active minds that had surrounded me were gone, and I stood at the window overlooking the University grounds where some of the younger boys were playing soldier.

It was the beginning of the term and Master Wiley, their captain, was drilling his new recruits, his boyish voice ringing out loud and clear as he walked beside his company issuing orders. His efforts to assume the dignity appropriate to his position, and the grave, stern look which his merry face was trying to wear, brought a smile to my lips as I watched him. Just then one of the elder pupils came into the room behind me and said, " A gentleman down-stairs wishes to see you, Miss McBeth." I replied, " Yes, Walter, I will go, where is he?" "In the reception room," and I followed him down the broad stairway, little dreaming as I passed into the room, that I was stepping across the threshold of a new era in my life.

Mr. Junkin, the gentleman who awaited me, was an elder in the church in Fairfield. I had often seen him in his seat on Sabbath, but he lived some miles distant in the country, and I had seldom met him in the year which had elapsed since I came to the University. " I received a letter from the secretary of our Board of Foreign Missions," he said after the first greetings were over. " It contains something that concerns you. Will you read it ? "

The letter read as follows : " I would be glad if you would see the Miss McBeths at once and ascertain their views about going to Tallahassee. If they think favourably of your suggestion, I would like for them to make application for an appointment at once. This matter requires dispatch as it is very desirable that whoever goes should be on the ground at least by the first of October. Let me hear from you with as little delay as possible."

" How did Dr. L—— learn of me ? " I asked, when I had finished reading the letter.

" I told him of you," said Mr. Junkin. " Years ago I was a missionary among the Indians myself and became very much attached to them, as I know you would also if you should go among them, and I am still deeply interested in these missions. Some time ago, knowing there was great need of labourers among that people, I wrote to Dr. L ——, telling him of you and your sister, Miss Kate, and informing him that if you would go, you were in my judgment well fitted for the work. I had no opportunity of seeing you before I wrote, and hope you will pardon me for doing so without your knowledge. The open letter was still in my hand, my heart and brain were busy with its contents, with myself and with the question so unexpectedly forced upon me.   The first of October, and this is the first week in September, less than a month, my heart sinking and quailing at the thought of leaving home and friends, to go to an unknown home in the wilderness, perhaps never to return.   Could I do it?" " Oh, no indeed!   Mr. Junkin, it is impossible," I said hastily, " not now at least.   My sister has gone home to Ohio, she would not go with me, I know, and I have entered into a new engagement with the principal of this institution; he could not supply my place in that short time, and it would not be right to leave him, besides I cannot leave my boys here," I added, as Captain Wiley and his band came in sight through the open window, and beyond them I caught glimpses of dear familiar faces, among the students scattered through the grounds.   " Oh! no, I do not need to go among the Indians to work for Jesus, I can find more than I can accomplish here.   Please tell Dr. L—— I cannot go at present."

When Mr. Junkin had gone home I walked slowly to my room, trying to convince myself that I had done right.   Once again in my own quiet room I walked to the window and stood looking out for a time unconscious of surroundings in the whirl of busy thought that filled my brain.   I looked around me, it was a very lovely picture that met my eye.   The beautiful western town with its tasteful homes standing back from the broad streets amid flowers and shrubbery.   The park, with its pleasant walks and shade trees, the church spires outlined against the sky, the University on a rising ground on the edge of the town, while beyond and around as far as the eye could reach, stretched the undulating prairie, dotted with white farmhouses and carpeted with its brilliant colouring of autumn flowers. Then, as sounds of music and dear familiar voices came floating up through the halls, my thoughts came back to the friends whose love made life's labours so light.

Could I leave them to live among the scarce civilized tribes of the forest? And yet who left a home in heaven for me—left His seat upon the throne of the universe to die for sinners? Was the servant above his Master? Might not the interview just closed be a call from Him? and I had decided and refused without even asking His will. If the call had been to go to India or China, I would have thought less of it, but the American Indians, a race in whom I had always felt such a deep interest. How could I slight their claim?

Even as I stood there pondering the subject, there came before me the memories of days when I had played upon the banks of the beautiful Ohio River which flowed before my childhood home. How distinctly I remembered sitting upon the huge rocks on the shore and examining the hieroglyphics, traced, as was supposed, by the red men when their tribes possessed the land. I recalled the deep sympathy I felt for the vanished race and longed to be a woman that I might go to the handful that yet remained and tell them the story of Jesus and try to show them the way to a home in heaven from which they could never be driven. Now I was a woman, the call had come and I had refused. "You have done wrong," said conscience. "But I have so much work I can do for the Master here, I do not need to go so far to seek it," said the flesh. "Fifty could be found to take your place here, to one willing to go to missionary grounds," urged the inward monitor, "and there is such great need for labourers in the field." And so the battle waged until the sun went down behind the beautiful banks of clouds that grace his setting in prairie land, and I turned to meet my friends, but the battle begun that night lasted for days. More and more distinctly as I prayed for guidance, came the conviction that I had done wrong, that it was my duty to go and labour with them for the Master for whom, as well as for myself, He died.

Before the month closed I wrote to Dr. L—— putting myself at the disposal of the board, if I was needed at the beginning of the year. By the last of January a letter of instructions reached me from Dr. L—— saying, " Your services are very much needed at the Good Water Female School among the Choctaws, Indian Territory, and we have appointed you to that place. It may be necessary for you to travel without an escort, so that your independence will be put to the test at once ; it will be for you to determine whether you can go alone. The route by St. Louis is by railroad to a place a little beyond Jefferson City, where you will take the regular stage route to California as far as Boggy Depot, ten miles from Wapenukka, our mission station among the Chickasaws, then on to Good Water. Let me know your decision at once." My friends objected to a stage journey of three or four hundred miles, thinking it beyond my strength, and by their advice I went to Keokuk, and after a short visit with my friends, the McQueens, I proceeded to St. Louis by rail, then down the Mississippi to the mouth of the Arkansas, then up that river to Fort Smith, finally reaching my destination.

She remained among the Choctaws until the breaking out of the civil war.

Miss S. L. McBeth came to Lapwai in the fall of 1873, and went up to Kamiah in the fall of 1874, after Mr. Spalding's death, and took up the work which he had laid down. That was, the preparing of young men for church work. Her first class consisted of the following persons: James Hines, James Lawyer, Archie Lawyer, Robert Williams, Mark Williams.

MISS SUE McBETH'S SCHOOL ROOM AND HOME IN KAMIAH

They met in a little log house belonging to the
government, where she began her work. She worked
in no haphazard way. She always had a plan to work
up to. Her experience as a missionary among the
Choctaws in the Indian Territory helped her now.
She understood Indian character, even then, quite
well.

She fully believed there could be no Christian citizenship in any tribe, until the tribal relations were
broken up, and that churches could not long exist that
were not established on the purity of the home. The
two objects to be attained were clearly before her.
The first, the power of the chiefs over the people must
be broken, and the man must feel his individuality,
instead of feeling he was a part of a band. Second,
the moral tone of the people must be raised.

In her early days in Kamiah, she found great intellectual pleasure in digging around the roots of the
Nez Perces language, a language formed according to
well established rules. Where did it come from?
She also enjoyed translating the dear old hymns into
Nez Perces. She was then as perfectly isolated as if
she had lived in Africa. The post-office was seventy-
five miles away. She took great pleasure in watching
the development, mentally and spiritually, of her class,
and in strengthening the church of Kamiah.

So she worked away, until the Joseph war, of 1877,
put a stop for a time to her delightful occupation.
Although the Christian Indians of Kamiah had noth-

ing whatever to do in the war, Joseph and his band were as bitter against the Christian Nez Perces as they were against the whites. Skirmishing was going on in that upper country, causing a great anxiety for the loyal Nez Perces, as well as for the whites there. Two or three white families were in the valley, who were connected with the government work.

Spies from the Joseph band often came in among the Kamiahans, to influence them to join the rebels, or to find out who were favourable to them. The story is told that some of the rebels intended to kill Robert, the minister in charge of the church there, who had influenced the people to be loyal to the government, but on surrounding his house, they heard him praying for them, and quietly went their way.

The battle of the Clearwater, the great battle of the Joseph war, was fought not many miles above Kamiah. Gen. O. O. Howard visited Miss S. L. McBeth in her little home, about a month before the war broke out, in the spring of 1877. His letter, describing his visit, was published soon after in the *Advance*, a Chicago paper. He says:

"In a small house of two or three rooms I found Miss McBeth, living by herself. She is such an invalid from partial paralysis that she cannot walk from house to house, so I was sure to find her at home. The candle gave us a dim light, so that I could scarcely make out how she looked as she gave me her hand and welcomed me to Kamiah. The next time I saw her was by daylight, which showed me a pale, intellectual face, above a slight frame. How could that face and frame seek this far-off region! Little by little the mystery is solved. Her soul has been fully consecrated to Christ, and He, as she fully believes, sent her upon a mission to the Indians.

" Her work seems simple. Just like the Master's in some respects. She gathers her disciples about her, a few at a time, and, having herself learned their language so as to speak it passably (this was in the early part of her work) she instructs them and makes them teachers.

" There is the lounge and chair. There the cook stove and table. There, in another room, is the little cabinet organ, and a few benches. So was everything about this little teacher—the simplest in style and work."

The trouble with the Joseph band became so great that the two white families in the Kamiah Valley spent one night in hiding. In a short time the command reached them from the agent, John Monteith, at Lapwai, " Leave Kamiah immediately." The getting out from such a place was no easy matter. They were on the other side of the river, with no ferry— only a useless flat-boat. The wagon to take them to Lapwai must be taken across the river in pieces, in canoes. When across, there was a three or four mile mountain to climb. These whites, Miss S. L. McBeth with them, were guarded from Kamiah to Lapwai by forty-five Christian Indians, and reached Fort Lapwai at five in the afternoon. They had travelled sixty miles in one day in a road wagon.

Miss S. L. McBeth shortly afterwards gave to each of the forty guards a memento of her gratitude in the shape of a picture. Years afterwards, when I entered their little one-room houses, I knew by these pictures that I was in the home of one of her guards.

Miss McBeth passed on down to Portland in rather a dilapidated condition so far as her wardrobe was concerned, but friends there soon made her presentable.

The Joseph war being over, she returned in the fall of 1877, to Lapwai, under commission from the Presbyterian Board of Foreign Missions, for complaint had gone on from the Catholic mission above Lapwai that she was doing church work under government pay. Up to this time, she had been in a sense under the government. Upon her return to Lapwai, the agent not thinking it wise for her to go to Kamiah at once, she called her pupils down to her home at Lapwai. Her class was somewhat changed then. Archie Lawyer and Mark Williams had been sent after the captive Josephs, as teachers to them in the Indian Territory. James Reuben, who was not of her class, was sent also. Others filled up the vacant places. She then had Robert Williams, Silas Whitman, Enoch Pond, Peter Lindsley, Moses Monteith, William Wheeler, James Hayes, and a part of the time, James Hines. Some others, also, who belonged to Lapwai, attended her school while she was there.

In 1878 Rev. G. L. Deffenbaugh arrived as superintendent of the mission, commissioned by the Presbyterian Board of Foreign Missions. Although a young man just from the seminary, during his nine years among the Nez Perces, he not only showed the gentlemanly, kind spirit of a missionary, among the people, but was a faithful leader of Miss McBeth's scholars into missionary work among the Nez Perces, Spokanes and Umatillas.

VII

THE JOSEPH WAR

Chief Joseph—Joseph War—His Flight—Bear Paw Mountain—
Capture and Surrender—Captivity—Sorrowful Hearts—Love for
the Graves of Their Dead—Their Return From Captivity.

CHIEF JOSEPH'S Indian name was Hin-ma-to-yoh-la-kit (The sound of the thunder coming up from the water). The home of old Joseph, the father of the warrior, was south of the Snake River. In the first treaty, made with Governor Stevens in 1855, his great domain was untouched, and old Joseph signed it with a good heart. But emigrants soon crowded into the country, miners especially. A new treaty must be made. A strip of land must be taken off the reserve on the north side of both the Snake and Clearwater Rivers, to give an unobstructed road to the newly found mines. Another treaty was made, in 1863, only eight years after the Governor Stevens treaty, by which not only was the reserve cut down, but the Wallowa Valley and region round about was excluded from the Indians' land.

Old Joseph was now in his grave. The mantle of authority had fallen upon young Joseph and his brother, Ollicut. Sometimes he was called young Joseph, also. These brothers were old Joseph's sons

94

by a Cayuse wife. By this second treaty the Nez
Perces tribe was divided into two bands, the treaty,
and non-treaty. Joseph refused to sign it, and was
soon joined by other bands. The White Bird band
was next in importance. That band roved over the
region of the Salmon River and its tributaries, without
any permanent abiding place. A band under the
command of " Too-hul-hul-sot " claimed the land between the Salmon and the Snake Rivers. That was
the chief who for his impudence was cast into prison
while the council with General Howard in 1877 was
going on at Fort Lapwai.

There was another band from Asotin Creek, and
still another led by Hush-hush-cut. They were a
roaming band in the region south of Lewiston, on the
opposite side of the river. General Howard thought
these bands, after they had arrayed themselves against
him, numbered about seven hundred men, women and
children. He says there were at least three hundred
and twenty-five warriors in the battle of the Clearwater.
They were defeated in that battle, in 1877, and fled
over the Lo Lo trail. There were no Christians with
them. Not many followed Joseph from either the
Kamiah or Lapwai communities, although great efforts
had been made to get the peace-loving Nez Perces to
join them. I think every one knows the story of
Joseph's masterly retreat over the trail, with many
difficulties on every side, for fourteen hundred miles,
fighting his way before three detachments of United

States soldiers, encumbered with the women and children and necessary baggage.

They were making a straight line—as straight as they could—for King George's land, Canada, to join Sitting Bull there. The settlers along his way were not molested. They only asked a passage, which was granted, of course readily, only hoping it might be a quick one. At length they reached Bear Paw Mountains, not far from British Columbia line, where they hoped to rest and refresh themselves, but a telegram had quickly told their whereabouts. General Miles came in on the other side, surprised, and surrounded them early one morning. They did not surrender without a struggle. Joseph's brother, Ollicut, and Toohulhulsot were killed there. Mark Arthur, then a child, was separated from his mother there, and did not see her face for eight years. Many who had been hunting their horses when the soldiers surrounded that camp fled to different tribes, and came straggling in to the home land by ones or twos for years afterwards.

The captives were taken on and on, till they reached Indian Territory. Many died on the way. Many died after they reached the " hot land," as they call Indian Territory yet. There they were given six hundred acres of ground to work. Two Nez Perces teachers and a minister were sent to them. Archie Lawyer, the minister, James Reuben and Mark Williams, the teachers. Mark and Archie did not stay there long on account of sickness. A church and school were started. Both seemed to be doing well, but the people were so homesick. There it was that Yellow Bull drank in his fevered dreams of the Red Rock spring. About this time Dr. George Spinning did faithful work to set these captives free. He said he counted the graves of one hundred children, and that all the children born there found their graves in that same hot land.

I think some of the people very likely died of homesickness. They have not the rebound in spirits we whites have. I have known some so depressed nothing could cheer them. Many graves were made there besides the graves of the little ones. At last, after eight years of captivity, they were released, and all who were Christians, or willing to take up civilized ways were allowed to come to the Nez Perces reserve. Those who were not willing, were taken up to the Cœur d'Alene reserve. Joseph and his reduced band were sent there. Joseph was always honest in his statement that his heart was just the same as it had always been. He had quite a band with him then, but it has dwindled down, from one cause or another, until now it numbers only about one hundred. Joseph died in the fall of 1904. Will they scatter since he is dead, or hold together under another leader? I think they will scatter. For a few years at first Joseph was afraid to come down upon the Nez Perces reserve—afraid of the surrounding whites, and because of the many indictments against him—but this fear wore off. Then he visited his friends—too often for their good, for he held to his heathenism with all the tenacity with which he has clung to his beloved Wallowa Valley. Never for a moment did his heart turn from his old home to the new one. The grave of his father was there. During the time of the allotment I knew of several who refused to take a better piece of land because of some graves on the old piece. " No, I must have the land where my beloved sleeps," was their answer.

Some whites think Joseph's body will be removed to the Wallowa. If this is done, it will be the first instance of the kind. I have never known anything like that before.

Joseph had one good thing about him. He was a temperance man. His visits year after year to Washington to get back his Wallowa have been truly pathetic. It is twenty-seven years now since it was taken from him. Strange that the government did encourage him to hope, even after that valley had been thickly settled. He refused to take land here, and kept many of his followers from taking theirs also. In one of his talks with President McKinley, Chief Joseph showed how he felt when he refused to sign the treaty. These are his words : —

" A man wants to buy my horses. I say, I no sell. He goes to my neighbour and says, ' Joseph has fine horses and I want them, but Joseph will not sell,' and my neighbour says, ' I will sell them to you.' So he comes back to me and says, ' I have bought your horses.' "

We could see the tender heart of the government when two years before all were liberated in 1885, a small band of women, widows, were sent home. Their teacher, James Reuben, wrote for the friends here to send horses to mount a certain number—about twenty—and to meet them at Kelton, near Boise, which was as far as they could come on the railroad. A number of Nez Perces started on that long journey with ponies. Some of the horses gave out. Others were sent for. For weeks before they reached the home land rumours were coming in that they were at a certain point. A few days later, still nearer. Somehow their progress was reported as they travelled along home. I happened to be in Lapwai when they arrived. The day that they were expected, I saw quite early in the morning groups of gaily dressed women sitting in little companies under the cottonwoods around the church. Yes, they were coming. Now quite near. Marshals for the day were chosen. Jonah, with his high hat and long linen duster, was the principal one. He, with a company of perhaps fifty men, started off with great dignity after dinner, intending to meet and welcome the captives on the top of Thunder Hill. Jonah soon returned, crestfallen. He said, " They are there. We met them.

But James Reuben said he would not shake hands with any one until he dismounted in front of the agent's office."

We knew then there was to be an imposing scene. They love ceremony so. And so it was. James appeared around a bend in the road, on a fine, fresh horse, and with a dark blue business suit on. Cartridge belt and pistol in its place! As free from dust as if he had but crossed the street! Where did he make his toilet? was the question. After him rode the weariest, dustiest, most forlorn band of women with blankets and belongings behind each woman on her horse. Two men besides James were with them. But the ponies! The poor ponies, after such a journey of perhaps three hundred miles! But they and the captives had been well drilled. A half circle was formed by them facing the agent's office. Their friends ranged themselves behind. James Reuben, from his saddle, with the oratory for which he was noted, made the opening speech, gracefully guiding his horse's head this way and that, as he addressed the now well formed half-circle. He pathetically described their sorrows in that far-off land, the hardships of the journey home, and the many they had left sleeping among strangers. The agent responded. James Reuben dismounted, drawing his horse's bridle over his left arm, leaving his right hand free to extend to his friends. Each captive did the same. Hundreds of friends gathered around, took

them by the hand, and oh! such weeping and wailing in remembrance of the graves in that distant land!
Doubtless there was great joy in their hearts, but just
then, the sorrow exceeded.

VIII

SCHOOL FOR WOMEN

Kate C. McBeth—School for Women—Learning the Language—
Soap-Making—Kamiah Church and Sabbath-School—The First
Christmas Tree—A Picnic—School at Kamiah a Year Later—Letter
Written in 1880.

I ARRIVED in Lapwai under commission of the
Presbyterian Board of Foreign Missions, in October,
1879, six years after Miss S. L. McBeth came.

Soon after my arrival, we two sisters moved to
Kamiah. Miss S. L. had been absent from that place
something over two years. We occupied the Spalding home for the first year in Kamiah, my schoolroom for the women being in the old government
log house in which General Howard had visited Miss
S. L. McBeth.

What an event the opening of a school for the
women was! At that time the moral standard was
low indeed. Although the old long tent, or long
house, had been discarded, they were not yet set in
separate families, too many still huddling together
into a one-room house or tent. Tripping and stumb-
ling into sin was a common occurrence, even with a
professing Christian. Of course, the session of the
church must follow directions, and forgive the peni-
tent to the seventy times seven! Miss S. L. McBeth

thoroughly understood conditions. She " finished her
mind," and decided that the breaking of the seventh
commandment would expel or keep out any offender,
and like her countryman, John Knox, she knew no
compromise. She often said to me, " We will not remember or consider the heathen past—only their walk
since they professed Christianity. The most of them
who wished to enter our schools were church-members,
and for fear that through ignorance injustice might be
done to any of them, she placed her school under the
care of the session of the church. Mine soon after
came under its care also, and at once one of my bright-
est and youngest women must step down and out.

Miss S. L. McBeth often said, " Help any one in
domestic and in spiritual matters, but a book must
not be put into the hands of a dishonourable woman,
thereby giving her influence, or power, among her
people for harm."

The desire of the people to know and to read were
so great, she knew she could draw the lines tight, and
still have good schools. All this, at the time, looked
very narrow to me. I was in such a hurry to lift all
the women up. It was not very long, however, before I saw their condition needed heroic measures.

It was discouraging work to get the standard
higher, but I found it could be done. Years afterwards, when I was living at Lapwai this was shown.
There at Lapwai was a native minister assisting Mr.
Deffenbaugh. His wife had been in my Kamiah

told the next day in the schoolroom, with the remark, " I was glad it was not drowned, for Miss Kate would have had to pay for it." (I have always been " Miss Kate " among the Nez Perces. My sister was " Miss McBeth.")

The soap was made and each woman carried her portion of it off in a little bucket, to dry in the sun. I said, " If any woman will get the grease, or meat rinds, ready, I will go to her home and see that she gets through the soap-making all right." Mrs. Kentuck was the only woman who accepted the offer. Of course she would have all the soap to herself. Pretty soon afterwards she named the day. I had a white friend with me that day. We found Mrs. Kentuck's house nice and clean, and the whole skin of a pig hanging up waiting for us. She had killed the pig herself, for the occasion. I found upon inquiry that the rest of them had no soap grease.

How cold that winter was! And only one board between me and the weather! In the spring I papered the board house with New York *Observers*, and nice and clean it did look. The white margin neatly matched looked just as beautiful in our eyes, as do the gilt figures on the walls now. (I liked the *Observer* because the sheets were so large.)

I was with the people in all their gatherings— whether Sabbath day or week days. I have a picture of the Kamiah church as it looked to me then, before me now. Fine looking men to the left of the pulpit, elders, and pupils from my sister's school. The session of that church was taught in her schoolroom. There elders were in the church, with white shirts and fine clothes on—mostly from missionary boxes, but worn with the dignity of the original owners—perhaps more.

Glancing on down the side seats, I had no trouble to see that they had arranged themselves according to their social—or rather, their spiritual, condition. It is just the same now in any of their churches. If the heart is not right with God, or if they are backsliding, they gradually slip farther and farther back, and, if the Spirit does not restore them, they do not stop at the door.

" Did you see where that man has taken his seat for the last few Sabbaths ? " is sometimes the question. They cannot put a bold front on, and cherish sin in the heart. I am glad they cannot.

As I sat that first winter in the Kamiah church with them and saw their enthusiasm and fervour in worship, I said, " This cannot last. It is all so new to them." The singing is different from the old heathen chanting. " We will see. It is but a few years since that great revival in the Kamiah camp."

Twenty-seven years have passed since, and they are the same to-day. Their hearts are still all aglow. Rain or shine, they are in their places on the Sabbath, and at prayer-meetings still. Not only in that church, but it is so in all the six churches among the Nez Perces. " All hail the power of Jesus' name ! "

Peter, the miller, a skeptic in Kamiah, who had known them in their heathenism as well as in their Christianity, used to say—" Religion means something here. It is good for the Indian."

Not long ago another white man, an Episcopal minister from Lewiston, was seeking for members of his flock. He found them mixed up with the Indian allotments on the Nez Perces prairie. He said to one of them, " How do you get along with these Indians? What kind of neighbours do they make ? " " Oh ! all right," was the answer, " only they are crazy on religion."

Yes! " Crazy," because they are devoted to their own church and attend its services regularly !

THE SABBATH-SCHOOL

In my first year in Kamiah, 1879, the Sabbath-school was started. The weekly study of the lesson, the systematic stepping from one important doctrine to another, has done much for the Nez Perces. The Sabbath-school means the congregation. All the people just keep their seats after the morning service.

When I began to teach in the Sabbath-school, I did not allow myself to stammer through, but wrote down carefully what I wanted to say, and translated it, before I stood before my class.

REV. ROBERT WILLIAMS

First Ordained Minister to Nez Perces

Pastor Robert Williams was the superintendent, the pupils from our two schools the teachers.

There was not room in the body of the church for the children's classes, so the children sat in a row, all around the pulpit platform, on the steps, and on the platform itself. Such a crowd of little ones, with their bright eyes gazing at the congregation, not only during the Sabbath-school time, but throughout the morning service, for they would sit there when they came in in the morning.

The " slips " of the big boys were soon exchanged for some kind of boys' clothing after that Sabbath-school began. The mothers were anxious to have their children appear well before the people.

·Only fourth of July (1904) while I listened to the after-dinner speeches at the camp-meeting, among the speakers a well-dressed, advanced man said, " I never had pants on until that Sabbath-school began at Kamiah, and then, my first pair was made out of a flour-sack, with the word 'Idaho' printed in large letters, on it."

Old Elder Billy had a class and made a good teacher, even if he could not read. He did not come with the teachers to my schoolroom on Friday, but never failed to slip in some time during the week to have me tell him about the lesson—if possible, put it in story form.

The Sabbath-school has lost none of its original interest after all these years have passed. This is true not alone of one but of all the churches. Of late years the English singing has added much to the interest, with Miss Mazie Crawford as the leader. They delight to sing either English or Nez Perces hymns.

In 1879 came gifts for the first Christmas tree, from friends in Brighton, Pa., and Steubenville, O. Now they are sent from Oakland, Cal., from Washington, Pa., and from Milwaukee, Wis., also. The tree was made more beautiful with garlands of popcorn and little tapers. When all was finished that Christmas morning, we locked the door and went home. All the afternoon we could see men and women go up and try the door, and walk away disappointed. At last, I saw a woman in the distance coming towards my home, in the deep snow. I soon knew it was Obia. I met her anxious face at the door, and the question to me was, " When will that good worship begin ? "

What happiness ! What joy ! to the people as well as to the children, there has always been at the Christmas time, and what a picture they made—the women with the babies, sitting on the floor in front of the tree. It would have hurt the mother's heart, if a little present had not been handed to her on the end of a rod or pole, over the heads of the other women sitting there, and the long Indian name of her child, which was found on a card attached to the present, called out by one of the dignitaries of the church. It was not only the Sabbath-school children, but every child in the community that must be remembered. Sometimes it was only a few threads of bright yarn, or an empty hairpin box. There was no offense if the child's name was not overlooked.

The next step in the progress was a picnic. I talked this over with Robert, the pastor. He said, " We will try that when the berries get ripe in August," meaning the black and huckleberries. When the time came for him to make the announcement, a picnic was hard for him to describe. No wonder—when he, himself, knew so little about it. He told them they were to take their food and spend the day at a cold spring on the hill or mountain eight or ten miles away. Any one could go that wanted to. He saw a perplexed look upon their faces and said, " It is just like fourth of July, but if you do not want to go— stay at home, and be silent," suiting the action to the word by putting his hand upon his mouth. Gestures and words go together very gracefully.

When the day came, all were there, not a lame, old man or woman absent! I rode a pony just like the rest of them, and when fording the river, called out to Mary and Abraham, " Catch my horse. It is backing so." " Look up," was the answer, while they caught the bridle and led him over.

The week before that picnic two large snakes made me a visit. I might say, they were in my house, for the wood-shed, where I saw them, was attached to the house. I had to pass through it to go into the back yard. The larger of the two got away. The other one was killed—but not by me. Its age was " nine rattles and a button." I had an exciting story to tell my sister, who said, " You had better not talk very much about them. The people will say the Te-wats (medicine men) sent them." I found out she was right, for many serious-looking men and women came to me on the picnic-ground, to inquire into particulars. With shrewd looks and nodding to each other they said, " It is the work of the Te-wats. They want to frighten her away'and so break up the women's school." I laughingly said I was not afraid of the Te-wats. A very reckless expression, they thought then. They are away past such superstitious fears now. The Christians, I mean. The Te-wats still have some power over the wild ones.

The whites speak of wild Indians and Christians. The Indians classify the whites in the same way, Christians and wild whites.

But what a place for a picnic! On the side of a steep, rocky hill. Sure enough, cold water! Too cold to be enjoyed!

The picnic did not become an established thing. There was a fear from the first that the " wild ones " from other places would gather, also, and so bring disgrace upon the church. The very next one brought trouble. We were enjoying the nice grounds, a different place from the first one, when we heard a pistol shot. Then all was commotion. A police from Lapwai had suddenly appeared to arrest a man, for some

cause. The man's friend sprang forward to help and
was shot. Nine Pikes did not die that day, but he
was taken from the picnic-grounds to his grave.

There have been picnics since, but with no great
sounding of trumpets beforehand.

THE SCHOOL AT KAMIAH A YEAR LATER

A little geography, arithmetic, spelling, writing,
singing, and much Bible-reading was the routine of
each pleasant day, for the knitting, cutting and fitting,
with the baking, came in the first year.

In our reading we followed the children of Israel
through their temptations and discouragements of the
wilderness way. My pupils were reading their own
souls' history, and they knew it. The sinning and
repenting, wandering and returning, was, and is, theirs,
as well as ours, the difference being that among these
people, the wanderer is made known by his return to
the blanket and long hair worn by his heathen friends.
Only one of our Kamiah church-members wears these
emblems now.

David's interesting life was also eagerly studied, one
of the precious psalms being read each day by a good
translator—and, from the closing prayer which followed
it was evident to even my dull ear, that the faithful
Spirit was the teacher.

I had much to encourage me as I watched the
change in their manner to each other, constantly
guarding against selfishness and jealousy. Even Mrs.

Kentuck, who used to look so black at Mark's wife (remembering past wrongs), has during the last months almost daily lifted the te-kash, with the dear little baby in it, put it on her old enemy's back and opened the door for her to pass out.

William Wheeler's new wife made great progress in her studies during the year, William helping her much in the evenings.   Martha, Silas Whitman's wife, has been able to teach her much about housekeeping. The Wheelers and Whitmans were our missionaries among the Umatillas.

IX

NEZ PERCES CHIEFS

The Chiefs—Nez Perces Laws—Persecution of Rev. Robert Williams
—Division, and Second Kamiah Church Formed—Scenes in Kamiah
Church, Sabbath-School and Other Services—A Second Letter.

IN July, 1880, the treaty expired, and with it chief-
tainships—virtually—as there was no longer any ap-
propriation by the government for the chief's salary.
Felix Corbett was the last one to hold the office. Not
that the chiefs were all dead—for they were standing
around thick, in Kamiah—more there than in all the
rest of the tribe. They were not all hereditary, nor
all made according to law. The time was when ten
scalps made a chief.

The seed royal at Kamiah would not down, but were
ready on all occasions to assert their superiority.
Some of this class at the close of services in the church
were prone to arise and harangue the people, thus as-
serting their interest in and care for them. Now the
minister in the Kamiah pulpit, Robert Williams, the
first native ordained (ordained in 1879) had not a drop
of royal blood in his veins. He was a fearless, out-
spoken man—uncompromising with the old heathenism—ever and always for citizenship. The disposition of many of the people was to mix up some of the

old ways with the new religion. Even when they said:
" Oh ! there is no harm in this or that old way," his
constant teaching was, " Throw away every bit of the
old." Because of his stand, he was the storm-centre
for years—the target of the chiefs.

After the government abolished the office of chief,
the Indians had a court of offenses, or court of justice, something on the plan which Jethro suggested to
Moses, where all the minor troubles might be tried,
and only the serious ones to go before the agent. The
chief of police was the important judge. Those were
the days when the well-paid, well-uniformed police
were to be met anywhere. Indians are born police-
men. What they cannot ferret out, no one can. They
had a small salary, which in the eyes of the poor people was a great one.

The session never appointed the one police who
patrolled the church grounds in Kamiah on Sabbath
day, but it was a place to show authority, and they
were very lordly. At one time an ex-chief was the
chief of police, or judge. That fearless pastor of the
Kamiah church was called before him, tried, and fined
one hundred dollars, " for the sins of his heart "—
there was no act charged against him. The woman
who testified against him said he had told her, such
thoughts were in his heart, but he had been hindered.
Of course, he never paid his fine.

The Blue Laws of Connecticut would pale before
such a court of justice, as there was in Kamiah then.

At another time, charges went to the presbytery against Robert Williams. He was tried and silenced for six months, for " Imprudence." The trial closed towards evening, in the Lapwai church. Mark Arthur, a young student, got on his horse and made a bee-line for Mount Idaho, sixty or seventy miles distant, to tell the anxious, little " white mother " there, Miss S. L. McBeth, the result.

" Imprudence! Imprudence! " He carried the word safely through, but what did it mean? was the question with him.

The papers from that presbytery containing the written testimony, were examined, explained and laid before the next presbytery, which sent up one of its members to reinstate the Kamiah pastor, more than a month before the term of six months had expired.

Those presbyters were honest, conscientious men. The truth is, an Indian plot is too much for the white man, and yet, an Indian is very often called " a child."

What a struggle before the chiefs would take their places as common citizens. Indeed, the wild ones yet talk of chiefs, although more than twenty years have passed since the chieftainship was abolished. The difficulty in Kamiah resulted in the formation of the Second Church of Kamiah, with the river rolling between the old and the new. At once, the new church chose Archie Lawyer as its pastor. This split in the Kamiah church came a few years after we sisters had left there, Miss S. L. McBeth for Mount Idaho, and I, for

Lapwai.   The division of the dear, old Kamiah First
Church was, as is always the case, a source of sorrow
to the mother church, but peace had been restored.
The community was large enough for two churches,
and friendly relations now exist.

The pastor, Robert Williams, has long since passed
over to his reward, and so has Archie Lawyer.
Archie Lawyer died in 1893 and Robert Williams
in 1896.

The Kamiah Church

The following letter, written in 1882, gives many
particulars.

How I wish you could see the people gathering
from far and near Sabbath morning, to the little, white
church over there among the pines, with the near
mountains for a background! No wonder that
Solomon, the stately elder, calls it the temple.   Many
of them come eight or ten miles—some sixteen from
their homes and, always at communion seasons,
Bartholomew and his band, come twenty miles.   The
people are there in time, too, Sabbath morning, for
they love to sit in squads on the grass in summer
time.   They used to sit in the snow, all the same, for
then no woman entered until the bell rang.   I am
happy to say, they are past that now.
They usually reach the church in companies, riding
their pretty, little ponies.   The men among them
have bridles and saddles made by white men.   The
women usually have a bright red blanket strapped
over the home-made saddle.   A long, plaited, hair
bridle tethers the pony to some of the little pines in
the foreground of the church.   The women, all with

gay head-handkerchiefs and bright shawls or blankets, make a bright picture.

It is a pleasant and hopeful sight to see the young families pass, the mother is very likely to have a child before and another behind—the one behind, tied to her just back of the saddle. The gospel is setting them in families.

The companies pass me on their way to church, with a " Good-morning " from men and women. I am sure to get a smile from the children, for I am associated with their Christmas trees and Sabbath-school, of which they are all members, except the wee ones in the mother's arms. Then they see the roll of Sabbath-school papers. That helps to bring the smile.

By the time I get to church these smart mothers have untied their children and all are down upon the ground and have tethered the ponies, then sent the older ones in and up to where all the Sabbath-school children sit, and the mother has already taken her place on the floor of the aisle—baby in her lap—for very likely every seat is filled when she enters.

The policeman in his uniform patrols the grounds outside until he is sure all are within. Not that there is the least need of it, but the policeman's office is a dignified one, and since the chieftainship is done away with, this comes next.

One of the elders stands inside the door—leaving his post at times to perform the duty, not strictly of usher, but packer, for after the seats are as full as full can be, then the floor is used. He can quickly see if any woman is using more of that than is necessary. If so, she is told or motioned to, to move over. If it were not for this usher, the door would be packed shut, also. Many a time I have stood in the little opening near the door, and wondered how I was to get to my reserved front seat. There was no way but by stepping over knees—the feet are under them, or as nearly as can be.

Now they have arranged themselves according to their social position, the elders and honourable men at one side of the pulpit, or near the front. It is near the door that the long hairs, and blankets, and wild eyes are seen. The middle block of pews and those on the other side are filled with women—my women and other honourable women to the front. Children are seated at the side of the pulpit, on it, and all around it. You will readily see the women form about two-thirds of the community, all that and perhaps more in importance, for whatever the women of other tribes may be, the Nez Perces women have their say in almost everything. They are bright and energetic. More energetic than the men, and would a little rather not hear the doctrine that the man is the head of the woman. I might say, they have their own way in the household.

Now many of the poor women sitting there on the floor are discarded wives. It is both amusing and touching to hear of the troublous times when the gospel gave but one wife to each man. I can see a reason now for so little hand-shaking and sociability between the men and the women. Minister and elders can look around upon old wives. Solomon thinks he must have had one hundred, but they are not good in figures.

There is no looking around to see who is coming in. All things are done decently and in order there. Our pastor, Robert Williams (Billy's eldest son) enters the pulpit and conducts the services with the air of a doctor of divinity.

How I wish you could hear them sing in their own language. They have sweet voices and sing in a minor key. The short spirited sermon, prayers and singing are in their own language. If they enjoy the sermon, or endorse the prayers, we often hear them respond with, " Aah."

This service is followed by Sabbath-school, but not until the men near the pulpit have shaken hands with the pastor and each other. A little arranging of classes is necessary, but they must sit to the front, for the congregation will keep their seats for this, to them, intensely interesting service. The teachers are, of course, from our schools, men and women. They have studied their lessons on Friday in the schoolroom— the very same lessons you use. They have no trouble in finding the place where the lesson is in the Bible, but oh! how the numbers in the hymn-book puzzle them. Sometimes they do not find the hymn until it is sung.

Now this little Bible and hymn-book the women carry in the pocket, wrapped up in a handkerchief, for in Sabbath-schools we always sing the English. The lesson is in both English and Nez Perces.

I have but to rise and turn around, and the most impressive scene of my life is before me, for there are the hungry faces of the whole congregation of women, looking at me from the seats and up from the floor of the aisle. Oh, what a helpless feeling often comes over me there with the store-house so full, and but crumbs falling through my hands to them! It is no wonder that I pray as I go and pray as I come, that the faithful, infallible Teacher may take the little and make much of it. Let it be your prayer, too.

While our lessons are in the Old Testament, it is not hard to take the chapters connected with the lesson and weave an interesting story from them. Imagine how thrilling David's eventful life would seem to us for the first time.

When Robert taps on the pulpit, how wide-awake the little ones look, and the people as well. It is a delight to hear the spirited questions, answered so promptly, often many answering at once. The teacher looks disgraced if no one in the class can answer. If the younger ones fail, the teachers are called upon.

I see a great change in the appearance of the children—more than in the people. How well I remember the big boy, in his slips, hiding behind his mother, from the " So-yap-po " (white).

The Sunday-school picture papers have a great attraction for them. How carefully I find them stored away in the rafters of their little homes. They are so eager to see what the picture is, and the pleasure is great, to the people as well as to the children. When I showed a little boy how to roll his paper nicely so as not to crumple it, the next boy rolled his the same way, and said with a beaming face, " Now, I am wise, too."

A short service and a sermon—preached by the pastor. Then the usual announcements are made for the evening (four o'clock). There are no after-night services. They live too far away. The ghosts are not all gone yet.

Three services are held at four o'clock, one up the river, one over the river, and one in the church. These services differ much from the others. After the opening hymn and prayer, a few remarks are made by the leader. The meeting is then open to any one. They call it witness-bearing. I call it, confessing their sins before God and to one another, or " showing their hearts." The presence of the Spirit is shown by the readiness to rise. Sometimes many of them rising at once. Most of them just talk on, no matter if there are others speaking, but a few of the more dignified ones stand, without any embarrassment, until there is silence. Usually the witness-bearing of each one occupies but a minute or two. Every now and then some one of the good singers strikes up one of their own sweet songs or hymns. To them, this witness-bearing is an important service. The spiritual condition of the heart is by it made known. A church-member who will not rise and show his or her heart, or bear witness, is looked upon with suspicion. Good Elder Solomon said once to me, " John has not spoken a word in prayer-meeting for a long time. Although we do not know of any open sin, sin is there, or his mouth would be open."

There is no such thing as a woman refusing to pray in the schoolroom, or in the prayer-meeting, and how direct their petitions are sometimes ! I heard this confession in prayer, from a man—" Oh ! Lord, Thou knowest to many of us heaven is far off and the horses are near." (They used to think so much of their horses, buying and selling and all that.)

Women as well as men take part in the prayer-meeting. Silence is guilt, and if it continues, the session will probe around to see what is the matter.

Are these people stoical ? Oh, no ! Just the reverse. I often see tears in the eyes of strong men. But they are slow to become excited.

Here is another letter written in the early part of 1884.

For some reason there has been an increased anxiety among the women this year for school. Among my new pupils were two young, married women,—one of them wore her first white-woman's dress into school. A queer schoolroom you would say. Fourteen women, two maidens, two little girls, and five babies for good measure, one of them a tiny one, two walking, two on all fours, making me watch my steps literally, for the mother's affections so centre upon the child, that to tread upon the little hand or foot would be all the same as upon the mother's heart.

How familiar the Nez Perces word " Pa-li-nin " has become as said by these mothers, for if they happen to lift their untrained eyes for a moment, they need guiding back to their place in the book.   It is well they are richly endowed with patience and persever-ance.   To be able to read the Bible in her own lan-guage is the longing of each heart.   To them, it is the book of books.   They receive all that come through it from Him, with such childlike faith that it is a great privilege to lead them into clearer light, and so strengthen these weak ones.

Our Sabbath-school still flourishes, as if of His own planting—profitable to old as well as to young chil-dren.   They often say, with beaming faces, " Aah ! taats ! " (Good is the Sabbath-school).

Doubtless many a Sabbath-school teacher in the East has been perplexed over the application of some of the late lessons—Paul's Letters to the Corinthians, while I have often thought if Paul had written to the Nez Perces, they could not have been more ap-propriate.   I can imagine from the expression on some of the faces before me, the question arising in their minds, " Who told Paul about us ? "   At the close of the lesson upon the burning of the sorcerers' books at Ephesus, our pastor said, " You know that was just like us at that camp-meeting over the river (in 1870) when the gospel came to us.   We brought out our Wy-ya-kins there.   What a pile of feathers and animals' tails, for they threw them all together and burned them, for all these men and women had an attending spirit of some bird or animal.

X

A JOURNEY TO LAPWAI

Camp-meeting at Lapwai—A Wedding—Nez Perces Missionaries Leave for Work Among Spokanes—Return from Lapwai—Camp at Cold Springs—Mrs. Felix Corbett's Feast for the "Stay-at-Homes"— Letter Written in 1884—Bread-Making, Sewing and Knitting.

IN 1881 we went down to camp-meeting at Lapwai. There religious services were kept up not only all day but far into the night. I liked to get up early in the morning, saunter along the high bank of the Lapwai to the little foot suspension bridge nearly opposite the agent's office, and from there watch the half-asleep people coming with soap, but no towel, to wash in the stream—perhaps wondering if they had been asleep at all. The very long summer twilight here makes the night very short indeed.

It was circulated in the camp that there would be a marriage in the school building in the evening, of a maiden to a young widower. The mother of the former wife got somehow into the kitchen and expressed herself with the volubility of an angry Indian woman. The fifteen-year-old bride-to-be was not able to hold her own with her. The sin charged was the throwing aside of the old custom, which was that the deceased wife's friends provide and make all arrangements for her successor. This they had not been given the privilege of doing.   Before the ceremony still another came and gave her views, so that when the very neatly attired bride stood before us in the school building, she did not have the air of a maiden marrying a chief's son.   The whites from the government school accompanied them to the evening service where they were given a very embarrassing position, on chairs in front. No wonder the young groom sat resting his elbow on his knee, for close beside him the former wife's mother sat, weeping aloud, piteously.

The sun sank to rest somewhere west of us, while Robert was preaching from that text which suits all colours, the Prodigal Son, and as it was the eve of the communion, wanderers were most tenderly invited back to the Father's House.   It is not so hard to distinguish the wanderers here, for the hair is allowed to lengthen and the blanket donned, when the heart loses its love for the Christ teaching.

If the Spirit moves, confession is made in the same public manner.   Then the prominent Christians step forward to give the returning prodigal the right hand of fellowship.   Such a thing as tasting the bread and wine with unconfessed sin is scarcely known among them.   Perhaps a little wholesome fear of man is felt as well as of God, for I have seen an elder quietly whisper in the ear of some guilty one who stood at the communion table, and the admonished one quickly slip down to the floor, without partaking.

The spirited sermon, singing, and prayers aroused

the spirit of the evil one in some wild heart who spoke from out a tent near, denouncing, in enraged tones, Robert and all that he said.

At the close of the camp-meeting I parted with my beloved Rachel who, with her husband, Enoch Pond, and brother, Robert Williams, took the trail, driving their pack ponies before them, up to the country of the Spokanes and neighbouring tribes in Washington Territory. How much I did want to go and see her new missionary field, but the long riding and camping out would have been too much for one not accustomed to it. Rachel and her husband will be there alone among a strange-speaking people. She is a bright Christian woman, and has her brother's ability as a leader. This, with her wifely and womanly qualities as well, fits her to be a teacher in the schoolroom and in the homes, also. Her own home, which has been for two years past near my house, was clean, bright, and cheery, and she so eagerly received and practised the instruction received in regard to it, that I often smiled and said, " The stream does sometimes rise higher than the fountain."

She has no children, so when Enoch was away, our evenings were often spent together, reading from the book the precious truth that in the person of the Son, one of us was as near and dear to the Father as the other.

The Sabbath-school will feel the loss of these men and women, but others will develop in the positions to which they are now advanced. What a blessing that Sabbath-school has been to women as well as to children in placing them side by side with the wise men. The study of our Sabbath-school lesson on Friday was always an interesting one, for those who did not teach were in my class on Sunday, and sitting beside them several who could not read but who liked to hold a book and gaze at the mysterious characters, pronouncing in low tones the words after the leader.

At Lapwai I saw Mrs. Deffenbaugh in her cozy little home. That is a very difficult part of the field, the contrast between the community there and at Kamiah being very great. There is much to contend with there—ungodly soldiers, horse-racing, whiskey and other evil influences from which Kamiah is free.

Going Home from Lapwai Camp-Meeting

After a week in camp we began our return journey. When three miles from the agency, we stopped at the garrison bakery, to add something more to our lunch basket, for we had a two days' journey before us, with the Indian driver to provide for. While there at the fort most of our Kamiah party passed us, three hundred men, women and children, and five hundred ponies. At the foot of the mountain, fifteen miles from the agency and near to the Catholic mission, we found them with camp-fires burning and tea and coffee-pot thereon, intending to rest and refresh themselves before beginning the toilsome ascent. In order to keep out of the dust, we started in our spring-wagon soon after lunch. By some means, one of the other two wagons passed us on the road (these three wagons were all there were then in the Kamiah community), and when nearly at the top, one of them broke down, giving us time to look back and down, and take in the picture of that living, moving scene as a whole. Afterwards, while riding through the twelve miles of forest which stretch from the top of the mountain to Cold Springs, our camping place, we examined the picture in its parts.

The women in companies, riding on the little spirited ponies, in bright, loose slips, with short, flowing sleeves, a handkerchief on the head, shawl pinned around the waist and riding man-fashion, hurried past, driving pack ponies before them on which were their good clothing, tent, and provisions, some of them not caring to be recognized in the native costume.

Occasionally there would be a three or four year old child, securely strapped into the saddle, whipping up its little pony to keep pace with the mothers.

The well-dressed men, with gray or linen dusters, broad-rimmed light felt hats, rode leisurely with slackened rein but erect figure, in twos, four abreast, or alone as they fancied, this side or that, enjoying the shade of the grand old pines. The ground there is as free from underbrush as a gentleman's park.

As evening drew on we were the last to enter the camp. Some of the tents were already pitched and fires kindled without. Because our baking was done at Lapwai, our supper was soon over, giving me time to sit on my wagon-seat and watch the doings about me. The men cared for the horses, while the women put up the tents and prepared the supper. All had warm cakes and the food of the whites, cooked in their own way, with many a can of sweets, bought while in Lewiston. By the time the much-enjoyed supper was over, night had thrown its mantle over us. It was easily done, in the ravine, with great trees about us. A bright fire of pitch-pine was made in an open space, showing where evening worship was to be held. The little bell was the signal.

Soon a half-circle was formed, the women seating themselves on the grass. The men stood, grouping themselves back of the leaders. Their sweet voices blended in praise to Him who had sought them in their darkness. A few words of exhortation, several prayers, in which our missionaries lately sent to the Umatillas were remembered, and, most tenderly, Robert, Enoch and Rachel, those to whom we had said good-bye at Lapwai. They had been part of our company going down, and were that night camping by a strange trail. Mr. Deffenbaugh had gone around by water and rail to the Spokanes.

After worship, Felix and Solomon, two of our elders, drew our wagon up near to the tent, spread blankets for our bed and raised the tent canvas over it. All was quiet and orderly in camp. We lay down—just sister and I, without a fear, with the double guard, a Christian people and the Angel of the Covenant, encamping about us. From out the tent I could hear Solomon telling Mrs. Solomon some of the incidents of their pleasant day at Lewiston, where they had been invited to share in the public feasts and festivities given in honour of the governor, who was present there on the Fourth of July. Two hundred Nez Perces in citizen's dress rode next to the liberty car, and had been treated with all the respect their dignity required, a dignity which forbade their showing surprise at anything they saw in Lewiston. That Lewiston has now a place in their hearts was evident from the earnest prayers which went up for the whole town from our church last Sabbath. Friends, individually and collectively, are always remembered there.

We might have slept soundly at Cold Springs but for the night watchmen, boys who herded the ponies a short distance from camp by riding round and round them all night, singing everything they knew to sing. The singing must have sounded sweet to the young bear that went up so near as to be caught by those noisy, happy boys.

The easy half of the way, thirty miles, lay before us the second day, and we were on the road as soon as worship was over in the morning, a treeless, rolling prairie, with a visible slope Kamiah-ward. The monotony of the way was only broken by the wild staring of the bands of frightened cattle or ponies. We made good time, for few were in advance of us when we reached the top of the Kamiah Mountain. From many a stopping-place on its descent of three or four miles we caught glimpses through the pines of the fields of waving grain in our own beautiful valley, and could imagine the welcome to be given to the weary travellers after nearly two weeks of absence, by the old women, or mothers of the little ones, who had been left to care for things generally on the little farms.

The ferry-boat was disabled, so we lunched in sight of home, and watched the ponies swim the swift river, and the wagons paddled over in canoes. We were so tired, we were quite indifferent as to which side of the river we camped on that night.

Early next morning one of my women, baby on her back, came to our house to tell of the happy Fourth of July the Kamiah women had. Mrs. Felix Corbett who had been left with her three little ones, sent old Barnabas, the only man on this side of the river, the day before the fourth, to every house, and invited all the women and children to a feast the next day at her house. A truly gospel feast it was, for the halt and lame were there, some of them riding ten or twelve miles. Sarah's description of it was, " We had plenty of sweets. The children had cherries. We all helped with joy, and all shook hands before we separated." This was the first woman's party ever known in the

tribe. Mrs. Felix had plenty to feast them on, and
being in the days of chiefs, a chief's wife, she knew
just how to go about it. No one is enjoying more
the pleasant remarks made upon it now than Felix,
who is only sorry that the fatted calf had not been
killed.

LETTER WRITTEN IN 1884 TO DR. LOWRIE, SECRETARY OF THE FOREIGN BOARD

For some time after your last letter was received
my head was full of what I would write to you, smiling
often at the idea of writing about such things to Dr.
Lowrie. The train of littles was suggested by the
sentence in your letter, " The domestic should not be
overlooked." It only shows you have the right idea
of the Indian question. Their ideas of labour and
dignity requires much patience to change—with the
male portion, at least—but to confine myself to the
women.

At times, when I look around and see how much
they have improved in appearance since I came, I am
much encouraged, but when I go into their homes, I
usually return with drooping wings, yet saying, " We
white women would not do any better with as little to
do with." I perhaps find some woman washing a dress
in a tin pan (not a large one) and giving it a squeeze.
Likely as not, when I show her a better way to wring
it out, she will answer, " I am wise now."

Their little farms provide the necessary food. They
are industrious in providing for the winter. Sister
says this is only of late years. They are anxious to
be dressed respectably on the Sabbath day, but beyond
this, few of them seem to care. I cannot see how
there can be much change until they take up larger

farms, and are helped to begin farming on a larger scale.

But you want to know about my school. I see there is even a greater anxiety to study and to read than before. Through the winter I had eighteen pupils, fourteen married women, two maidens, two little girls, and five babies. A new pupil came in last week—perhaps not a very hopeful one, for her husband is still in the blanket.

I wish you could have seen the look of intense interest on the faces of my pupils as they stood in a circle around my cook-stove while that emblem of sin was made—yeast. Only one woman took the offer which I made, that to any woman who would bring the corn-meal, I would teach how to make dry yeast. The making of this was a schoolroom scene. I did not need the cook-stove.

Just here a few words on the bread subject. Every woman who has ever been to my school, and some outside, have been taught to make yeast bread, and yet I am certain of only a few who have quite given up the time-honoured flatcake. Why? Oh! they have no hops, or nothing to keep the yeast in, or, they forget to make fresh yeast. They do not like care.

Each woman has a highly prized little book, with a recipe in it in which they have perfect confidence, for did they not see the whole process the day we had school in the kitchen? Then a just division was made of the cakes and snaps when baked. Each share went home to husband and children, tied up in the handkerchief with the gospel hymns and the Bible. Oh! but we must be patient until they adopt the white woman's ways.

Now, Doctor, in my schoolroom hang two wall-pockets full of patterns. Every woman who has ever been in school has had one or two dresses cut, basted, fitted, and a pattern of the same to take home for future use. Not only the women of the school, but every woman who wished to dress like a white woman, was supplied. Oh! how often, when I have been tired from the schoolroom work, have I seen a woman slipping around to the back door, and knew she had under her shawl material for a dress—but no linings. I do not forget the black look one of them gave me when I handed her the dress, cut and basted. Was I not going to sew it tight? There were no machines in those days.

The basting for them had to be done at first. If not, just as likely as not, and a great deal likelier, I would see that woman or that woman's child at church the next Sabbath, with the back gores to the front.

I am happy to say, this work of pattern-making grows beautifully less and less. It ought never to have been such a tax upon my time, and but for the native selfishness of my women—good women, but not willing to communicate their wisdom—it would not have been so heavy. I am not sorry now for this work. It is work that shows results.

All who have ever been in school have knit at least one pair of stockings; the yarn for the same, and needles, presented to them. They enjoy knitting. Some of them are speedy. This acquirement was not so easily kept under a bushel. I often find quite a number whom I never taught, knitting and getting the heel turned somehow. The men are very proud to show their wives' handiwork. I have heard of two of them, who while away at Lapwai, had something hurt their feet so badly that they had to take off their shoes or boots. They knew the bright stripes of their stockings would attract attention!

The subject of personal cleanliness needs here a little and there a little, all the way along. It is so easy to slip on a better dress on the outside, and then off to church. My women, too, are ready to listen to

all that comes from God. I hunted up what He said
on the subject of cleanliness—made it plain from references on the board that He was not silent about how
they should approach Him. Two of the best readers
translated. Then I gave each a little slip with the
reference to take home with them, that they might
read again and to others. How touching was the
expression in the closing prayer that day! "Oh!
Lord, please forgive us. We did not know that before." Docile as children towards Him.

Some of their expressions show the Light within.
In Robert's sermon last Sabbath, in holding up Jesus
as a tender, loving guide to His followers, he said,
"And you need not be afraid of the Father. He is
koup-kin-e-ki " (Just on the other side of Jesus).

I could have written a letter and have picked out
a few of my women as they appear on Sabbath and in
the home, and made a beautiful and a true picture, but
the impression from it would give you a wrong idea
of the whole.

The Sabbath-school is still an interesting service.
Four adults were baptized last Sabbath, our communion
day. When I inquired how many united with the
church, the answer was, " Four," although I had seen
five other young women. They were not counted.
They had been baptized before. This, I suppose, is
right—to look upon the baptized children of the
church as members, but not in full communion.

This short, happy winter has passed. Some of my
pupils have already gone back to their little farms, to
work through the spring and summer months.

XI

SCHOOL-DAYS IN KAMIAH

THESE, our first really fall-looking days, do not seem gloomy, for the mill is running after the long harvest rest, and the women are going to and from it, keeping their number and that of the meek-looking untethered ponies around the mill about the same all day. The government steam-mill is manned by white men, who with the family in the government school and ourselves, constitute the so-yap-po or white society of this eastern end of the reservation.

Harvest began the last of July or first of August in the valley proper, but where the farms lie above the foot-hills, even later. There is no need of a hay harvest here, where the bands of Cayuse ponies roam at will, and know how to scratch the snow from the bunch grass in winter. When hunted up and brought home in the spring, their sleek looks tell us that they have fared sumptuously every day. A few of them are then selected for home use, and the rest given their freedom again. Cattle are not so numerous, but live in the same way. There are no sheep. The coyotes, or little wolves, are too numerous.

The harvest was tedious, owing to the primitive mode of working. Much of the grain was cut with scythes—all swung by the men, who consider this their part of the work, even if it was, as some of them expressively put it—" too much warm."

The threshing was left to the women and was begun at once, on the field. Sometimes done by one woman alone, but oftener in companies, " neighbouring " as the men do at harvest at home. If they have a long stay in the field, they are prepared for it. The old tent is pitched there, even if not far from the house. On a skin sled the grain to be threshed is hauled to the skin threshing-floor placed in order where usually two women, each on her own pony and leading another, slowly ride the circuit until the grain is separated from the straw.

Then the winnowing—through a colander-like sieve, held higher than the head, and as the grain falls, a gentle breeze carries the chaff a little further. We know little of strong winds here. The mountains form a good, strong wall to ward them off.

The grain needed for family use and for seed is put into a we-kash—looking like a large dry-goods box. The rest is sold. The money obtained from the sale of their grain to the people in towns near and in the mines, and the packing to the mines, of whatever is required by the miners, provides the winter's supply of groceries.

As so little grain is stored, there is not much need

KAMIAH

of barns. All this harvesting has been done without the anxious looking skyward to which we are accustomed, for we have much less rain here than in the states. Strange that the ground is so moist and mellow.

CHRISTMAS CELEBRATED ON NEW YEAR'S

Why did we celebrate Christmas on New Year's? Not because the chiefs had their feast a week after Thanksgiving—made a mistake and had it then—but because on Christmas there were nearly four hundred swollen arms from vaccination in the Kamiah community.

It is not evening yet, but I must not wait until evening to take over to the church a parcel for the little girl who was quite forgotten until I met her father at noon, who asked if his girl was remembered on the Christmas tree. I did not think when I started that the pony parade usual at Christmas time would be back so soon, for the paraders had been up past our house, and waved and waved as they passed by, but just as I was going down by the mill, I heard them coming behind me—singing the same few words to the tune they always sing on joyous occasions—" I'm going home, to die no more!" So I stopped and got out my pocket handkerchief to wave.

How I wish you could have seen these fine-looking, neatly dressed men, on their spirited ponies as they came on a lope, two abreast, and as they passed, every hat lifted and waved, General Howard style.   Some of them had seen him do so once, and they are such perfect imitators, and never awkward under any circumstances.   Probably because they never feel themselves inferior.

Between the mill and the church, to the right, stood one long lodge.   Several tents were pitched there by the " distant ones," just for the Christmas occasion. No wonder, for it is the one only evening entertainment of the year, the people enjoying it quite as much as the children do.

A part of the riders had dismounted when I arrived, and were hitching their ponies in the enclosure near Joshua's little house, and from the way the smoke was hurrying through the lodge poles, I knew a feast was on the program.   Usually a feast means a council, and great subjects to be discussed—but perhaps not, to-day.   Not a woman was to be seen, but the children were all out.   Some sitting on fences—some standing with their little hands clasped behind them—perhaps wondering what was in my basket.   Quaint little girls they were, with their hair in four braids, dresses made with a belt, but longer than their mother's.

Now put in this picture any number of dogs, of all sizes and colours, for no Indian scene is a true one if they are left out.   To the left are the little pines which ornament the foreground of the church and serve as hitching posts for the little ponies on Sabbath.   The little trees are not hurt by it, for the riders all carry a long, plaited hair tether, done up like a clothes-line, and dangling from some part of the horse's saddle as they pass. When they alight, they slip a noose over one front foot of the pony, and fasten the other end near to the root of the tree.

Some stumps are burning, for although not a cold day, it is a damp one. Around one are some long-haired, blanketed braves, who are not allowed—because of the hair and the blankets—to ride in the procession. Is it not a strange thing, when they are so proud of their glossy locks, that not one of them will allow their beards to grow, but watch and pull out every hair.

At some distance, around another stump, are seated women on the wet ground, holding children in their laps. The dirty gray blankets of the older ones make the newer ones of the younger women look brighter. Poor, worn-out, old women! But they are talking over the past, perhaps like the dear grandmas at home, contrasting the then with the now.

Later in the evening, when the bell rang, I noticed them limping to the church. The children got in first, for they ran.

I thought, when this tree on the banks of the Clearwater is such an attractive sight to them (the old women), what will the Tree of Life on the banks of the River Clear as Crystal be to those of them who drop the blanket for a shining robe, for the Father's eye will rest lovingly on the blood of His Son, and honour it, even if found on the heart of an old Indian woman.

School-Days at Kamiah

Beautiful for situation is the site of the First Church of Kamiah.   But historic interest gathers around the little three-roomed box house, with its outside chimney, built in 1880 quite near to the church and shaded by the pines, for there it was Miss S. L. McBeth lived and wielded an influence felt in every part of the tribe, which is felt still, although the snows of thirteen winters have fallen upon her grave, near that little church, which was as dear to her as her right hand.   Out of that church came nine of the eleven ordained native ministers.   For dignity and importance it was like a college church in its palmiest days. Robert Williams, a native, preached in its pulpit as a student, and for seventeen years after his ordination— first as a supply, and then as pastor, until his death in 1896.

Miss S. L. McBeth, the faithful " little mother " in the little box house was always at home, to receive, to counsel and to direct these native ministers and their helpers in their work among the people.   This was a part of her plan that the natives should do the work in their assemblies.   Even in harvest time, the little ponies were seen, tethered to some of the little pines near her house, while the owner was receiving *him-tak-ash* (help), for some prayer-meeting or service he had been appointed to lead.

Her students were the pastor's helpers. I wish every native pastor could have such a nucleus about him. Prayer-meetings at different points in the congregation have always been kept up.

These men came to her with all their troubles and told her everything. They were sure she would sympathize with them—and how patient she was with even the dullest. Nothing that could benefit them was too small for her care—even teaching them how to hold the knife and fork, or how to drink their tea or coffee—teaching them also to care for their health, a much needed knowledge with them.

My sister's new pupils, after she went the second time to Kamiah, were Robert Parsons, Caleb McAttee, Williams Parsons, Stephen Axtell, Luke Williams, Mark Arthur, Felix Corbett, Solomon Whitman.

Truly the care of all the churches came upon her, although she seldom appeared in their assemblies. The atmosphere of the crowded church affected her weak lungs. Notwithstanding this they all knew her. Once seen, how could they forget that pale face, and the searching look from those hazel eyes.

The summer heat of the valley was hard upon her, so for a number of summers she spent a time in the cooler air of Mount Idaho. Finally, she bought a house and moved there. There was another reason for this. In those days the authority of an Indian agent was like that of a czar, and it was partly because the agent of the tribe threatened to remove us from the reserve because of her protest against some of his measures, that she went to Mount Idaho. One of his complaints against us was that we were creating an aristocracy among the Indians, and that he could not manage them as he chose. Christianity *was* then up-lifting a class, although they were about all alike poor.

Her pupils, with their families, soon followed her there and through the liberality of Mr. and Mrs. Wm. S. Ladd, of Portland, Oregon, and Mr. and Mrs. I. P. Rumsey, of Lake Forest, Ill., little houses were built for these students.

For the first two or three years after we went to Kamiah, there was a little government school there. Its capacity was only twenty or twenty-four. We found Mr. and Mrs. W. O. Campbell in charge. The memory of their kindness and helpfulness is fragrant still. They were called to Lapwai and Mr. and Mrs. McConville put in their places. They, too, were much help and comfort to us. When the government con-solidated the Lapwai and Kamiah schools at Lapwai, it took the McConvilles away, and the only white women left in the Kamiah Valley were just we two sisters.

The same fall of 1885 that my sister moved to Mount Idaho, a letter came to me from Rev. F. F. Ellinwood, D. D., Secretary of the Foreign Board, saying that I had better go down to Lapwai. The board would feel uneasy to have me in Kamiah alone. I might get sick there, with no doctor, and no white friends to care for me. (How vexed the people were to think that he could not trust me to their care !)

Great was my sorrow at thought of leaving Kamiah, and going down to Lapwai—that moral cesspool of the tribe—apparently a hopeless place to work in. The people of Kamiah then looked down upon those at Lapwai as inferior. Indeed the difference was so great that strangers often asked if they were not of different tribes. But all that is past, and now it is no disgrace to be of Lapwai. In those days, if a Kamiah man or woman was going to the bad, they wanted to move to Lapwai where they would feel more comfortable. The people at Lapwai had influences about them which were not uplifting—to say the least, the soldiers of the fort, the agency, and nearness to Lewiston. From all these Kamiah was free. Around an Indian agency in those days a company of hangers-on would be found, ready to take anything that was to be given. The Nez Perces were then receiving annuities for the land purchased by the government. These annuities were in the shape of wagons and farm implements. Some of the very old were receiving help in the way of food or clothing. I am happy to say, the Nez Perces never, even in their wildest days, received rations, in the sense in which the word " rations " is used. There was no ration day, when beeves were killed and the meat distributed to the hungry crowds standing around, who, by receiving it would cast away their manhood.

The six years I spent in Kamiah were profitable years to my own soul, at least. There I found out that happiness does not depend on one's surroundings. The Bible seemed to be a new book. I could see " wonders in the deep " in it. There I could wander around among a strange-speaking people, humming as I went —

> " I am as near as can be,
>   For in the Person of His Son,
> I am as near as He.

> " I am as dear as dear can be,
>   For in the Person of His Son,
> I am as dear as He."

In that valley, with the world shut out by high mountains, and we shut in with God, I would often think of a farewell meeting in my own home church, Wellsville, Ohio, in 1879, when Dr. Grimes rose and turning towards the eight ministers who had spoken, said, almost fiercely, " Sacrifice ! Brethren ! What are you talking about ! She is making no sacrifice. No ! The Lord will far more than make up to her all that she is leaving."

Truly, He did. The " Lo, I am with you always ! " was so real that at times I felt that by reaching out my hand, I could touch Him.

They were not all cloudless days there, for at times some real or fancied injustice of the white men would stir the Indians " from Dan to Beersheba," *i. e.,* from

Kamiah to Lapwai. Then again the internal troubles of the little church would send us to our knees.

My last Sabbath in Kamiah came. Robert announced that Miss Kate was going to leave them. He thought only for a time—and said perhaps she will come back. "She is not going far away—only to Lapwai."

I saw a sullen look overspread some of the little faces on the pulpit platform, where the children always sat, which was explained when I came to the door where some of the women were waiting for me. One mother held the hand of her little boy, saying, "Do you know what John says?" "Tsi-ou, Miss Kate, Tsi-ou, Christmas." (Absent, Miss Kate, absent, Christmas!) The little selfish hearts were saddened at the prospect of no Christmas. I said, "No, no. Christmas will be here all the same."

XII

THE SEMI-CENTENNIAL

THE day came for me to start to Lapwai. Many were going down. I had not much to move—the organ, a few boxes and my trunk. The rough home-made furniture was left for others to use.

The little shoeless ponies had hard work to gain the top of the steep mountain, giving me plenty of time to look back and down at the beautiful valley—none the less beautiful because I saw it through my tears. There, in sight was the old ground where Lewis and Clark camped, and, better still, the place where many became sons of God, born of the Spirit.

We reached Lapwai after two days and two nights on the road, because it was so muddy and bad. My heart was " a little one " when I rode up to the old government house near to the church that rainy evening in November, 1885. Mr. Deffenbaugh, his young wife and the people gave me a welcome. The agency buildings were in sight just across the way, but agents and their employees were not always in sympathy with mission work.

The new Lapwai church was not yet completed when I arrived. The first sermon preached in it was, I think, on January 8, 1886. The little treaty church, built by the government, had been removed across the road, and was used as a warehouse, and has since been destroyed by fire. The new house was erected on the old site, and how proud the people were then of it—and are still—because they built it themselves—not with their own hands, but with their own money, with a little help from the board !

The garrison was abandoned that same year, and the farm and buildings transferred from the War Department to the Department of the Interior, for school purposes.

In that year, 1885, the captives of the Joseph band in Indian Territory were liberated and the Christian portion of them allowed to return to the reserve. Joseph was not willing to take land here, and he, with some of his band, were sent to the Cœur d'Alene reserve. He lived there until September, 1904, when death came.

The new Lapwai church was not any too large, for many of the Joseph band found homes in the Lapwai Valley and increased the attendance there. Our now good Elder Whitfield was one of them.

My school for the women opened soon after I reached Lapwai. It was conducted much in the same manner as the school in Kamiah—perhaps a step in advance, for the sewing-machine was introduced.

How proud the women were to be wise in the use of it! The younger women helped their friends much. That one machine in the Lapwai Valley was kept busy for years, but just as soon as their payments came for the surplus land which the government had bought from them, the first things bought were spring wagons, American horses, and sewing-machines. This money was also used in building neat little homes, or in making additions to those they were using.

A Walk During the First Winter in Lapwai

From my home it was just a few steps down to the miller's house, but a white family lives there and I will not enter. Just beyond the mill is a little Indian home, but I will give you the description of that at the last. I pass by and find next a tent, the entrance so low no one can enter without doing obeisance to the inmates, face to the ground. Abraham could not have sat in that tent door with any comfort. The baby was the first to discover the coming of the pale-face, and gave the alarm in cries of terror. There are but few braves among the babies here.

I seated myself beside the mother on the skin floor and inquired the name of her husband. I could tell from the name if he were a professing Christian. Then she would be Mrs. Solomon, or the wife of some of the good and great of the olden times. She answered,

with downcast eye, " tsi-ou ha-mo " (no man). There
is no word in the language for *home* or *husband*.
"Who is father of your child?" I asked. "Tsi-ou
pisht" (no father), was the answer. The old woman
sat by the central fire, looking very mummy-like, and
no wonder, for doubtless much of her long life had
been spent in the smoke of the camp-fire.

A house of two rooms was near by. It had for its
regular occupants, an old man and woman, with granddaughter, her husband and three children. Oh! the
dirt, and odour of putrid flesh, fish and venison, drying
for the winter. The old woman began begging clothes.
Said her granddaughter would come to my school
if I would give her a dress. I said, " She can wash
the one she has and come on Friday. That is the day
I have my school in the kitchen, and I will teach her
how to make white bread." Soda biscuit and flat
cakes were all they knew about bread making. Of
course, that mysterious thing, yeast, they knew nothing about here yet. The answer came with an air
corresponding thereunto, " My granddaughter is wise
now. She knows everything."

The sequel to this visit might have been written
several weeks ago, when the old woman came to tell
me that a Mrs. Daniel had shown her granddaughter
how to make the bread of the whites, and she had
tried it three times, but it would not grow. Of course
not without the plant. She had had no yeast in it.

About the space of a field further on stands Joe's

little house. Such a funny, little, crooked one, with one light of glass for a window ! Mrs. Joe tried hard to talk to me, in broken English, or Chinook. She had many complaints to make about Joe. " Joe no marry me. Me have three children. They no baptized. Elders no let me take the Lord's Supper." Much wisdom is needed in giving advice to such persons. Her bright, happy face and merry laugh gave me the impression that she was not greatly troubled on any of these subjects. I left the little house, wondering if any white woman could make that dark little place look any better than she did, if in her place.

There was a tent and a house but a short distance further on, an old couple and daughter living in the tent, the son and the young woman occupying the wee, box-looking house, which was clean, however. This young woman wanted to enter my school, to which I answered, " Yes, when you are lawfully married to the man you are living with." We need to take a most decided stand on this subject, preachers, and teachers. They think the few words of the Christian marriage are not nearly so imposing as the old ceremony of bartering for the bride, and making presents afterwards.

But one more house to go to, for the mountain is now so close as to mirror itself in the river, and there is but a trail between it and the stream—the Lewiston trail. As I drew near, the old man came out, glad to see me. There was a well-to-do air about everything

there. The wagon shed sheltered many useful implements. The turkeys were walking around in the
young orchard. All this was very pleasant to see.
But, oh! the inside was such a disappointment, for
the young wife had been to the government school,
and we expected more. She and her husband were
living with the old couple, the old man highly respected
in the tribe, a stern-looking judge—his gray hairs adding somewhat to the dignity of his office. I can think
of only one other old man with gray hairs in the tribe
at that time. I stood on the little porch of that house,
looking over the river to a place of many tents, which
I knew must be where lived Jude's band, the Tse-
wek-ta, the same place where old Eagle lived. From
the porch I examined that Sinai-looking mountain,
and wondered under which stone he died. Two
women from this same heathen band pushed open my
schoolroom door a few weeks after, and stood, closely
examining teacher and her pupils. They did not
wish any favours, not even a pattern. They just came
to see.

My homeward way was close to the river. As I
walked along, I was contrasting Kamiah and Lapwai.
Of course, you would expect me to be doing that.
Strange that the river looked so much smaller here
than it did there. I contrasted the appearance of the
two communities with a heart-sinking feeling coming
over me and saying, "Who is sufficient for these
things?" Yet I do see the Lord has been making a

place for me in their hearts. With what kindly faces they have all met me, and cordial hand-shaking! For all knew Miss Kate, although she knew few of them. I never had greater longings for fitness to serve than now, and although the spiritual is never forgotten in our intercourse, the secular must have a place in all Indian work. There is much need of work for the mothers here. Some of them have daughters who will be coming home from the training-school soon, and they will have much to contend with on their return.

I reached the little Indian home by the mill, and here in young Mrs. Noah's house will rest awhile. Two men are here—father and son. All is so clean, and everything in its place. The bedsteads of rough boards, the chairs clumsy, and the family such a picture. The young wife, perhaps not twenty years old, the mother of a dear little girl of five, and a boy of two. The grandmother, a very young one, a widow indeed, completes this Christian household. Mother, grandmother and children have been in daily attendance in my school since it was opened this winter. They have beautiful faces. How often I have looked from the gentle children to the gentle mother and grandmother, and thought of what Paul wrote to Timothy, about the faith "that first dwelt in thy mother Eunice, and grandmother Lois." It might have been said the faith of thy mother Amelia, and grandmother Mrs. Timothy. How gracefully either of these women would don an apron and step around my schoolroom as teacher of something they had been taught the Friday before. What nice bread I have seen in this home!

Are you disappointed in this picture that I have made? The poor women here at Lapwai have never had any work among them. But few of them have ever seen into the home of a white family. I try to make mine as bright as possible. Noah's little home by the mill has some ornaments of their own making.

The next fall, after I moved to Lapwai, in 1886, was the semi-centennial of the mission, the fiftieth anniversary of the coming of Mr. and Mrs. Spalding to the Nez Perces. Very appropriate indeed it was that the memorial services should be held in the large new church. This was not a matter simply of interest at Lapwai, but to the whole tribe. It was not a very good time to hold it, in November, with the old people to come from a distance; but the most of them came. Mr. Deffenbaugh made out the program, which through the day was to be the giving of reminiscences by the old people, and the five evenings were to be spent in worship. How pleased the old people were, to be literally and figuratively, to the front. Each old person when called upon would come forward as if he were coming to the witness-stand. There had been much surmising from end to end of the reservation as to what kind of a meeting it would be.   Billy got the nearest to it, I think, when he said, " It will be just like a presbytery." He knew a presbytery was a delightful place.   He went sometimes as an elder, sometimes as a sightseer.

These exercises through the day and evening were kept well in hand by Mr. Deffenbaugh, leaving me free to take notes, of which I append some :

Billy said, " Our people used to worship the sun as our father and the earth as our mother.   At last a trapper, I am not quite sure who he was—think maybe he was a half-breed, told us about the true God."

Elder Paul's story was, " The first white man to tell us was the priest—perhaps near to where the Cœur d'Alene mission is now.   He told the Nez Perces how to worship as the Catholics did.   Many doubted if what he said was true, and for that reason they sent four men to inquire about the truth."

Elder Paul was the father of our present Elder Matt Whitfield.   Paul was a stout, heavy-set man, and a short time before this meeting had been made a judge.

Billy said, " The people used to be afraid of their priest—not Catholic priest.   They had a white pole. One priest, Ta-wish-wa-hickt, told them if they went near it they would die.   He told them to worship him, and give him everything he needed, and he used to tell them to give him a young girl for his wife, and they obeyed.   They worshipped by dancing around the pole.   The pole had flags on it.   We do not know where the flags came from.   It is hard to tell.   In their dancing they were careful not to go nearer than within two hundred feet of the pole."

Dear old Billy ! How he enjoys the light now.

Paul said : " They used to give horses or anything the priests asked for." The first-fruits were given them, also tithes, much as the Israelites used to do. How many of their old ways were like the children of Abraham !

Kamas, of Kamiah, marches up the aisle with martial tread and important air to tell where and how they knew about the white man and the white man's God. He knows his story is true. Then he gives the story of Wat-ku-ese in all its details. Wat-ku-ese was the woman who was taken captive and saw the first white people.

Billy again : " I saw many white men over in the Buffalo country, when I heard my cousin was dead."

Billy's cousin was one of the two younger men of the four who went to St. Louis.

Billy resumes : " I saw there Hi-yuts-to-he-nin who was one of the four. He came back alone. When I saw him he was talking with a trapper over there, one of King George's men. He called some of all the tribes to celebrate Christmas. That was the first I knew about Christmas."

Noah, the old elder of the Lapwai church : " I remember we went to meet Mr. Spalding. We met him opposite Lewiston. He told us he had come to stay. I think Whitman was with him."

Mr. Deffenbaugh here reads a letter from Mrs. Spalding to her sister, written, perhaps in the buffalo tent fifty years before. She calls the place, " this dear spot," and tells that the Indians carried the logs from the river four miles away for their house.

Noah says, " Horses were not wise. We had no harness, no anything. Mr. Spalding taught us how to make garden."

Billy remembered they used to sing the year, " Eighteen hundred and thirty-seven," and gets up and sings it. They sang the number so as to make the Indians remember the year.

James Hines was a boy when Rev. A. B. Smith was in Kamiah. He says he rode one of Mr. Smith's four horses when he began to plow. He took care, also, of the cow.

James Reubens's grandmother tells that they made brick, that they gathered grass and mixed it with the mud to make the brick. She said they made stoves in the same way. The old men say she is correct.

Then they tell of Governor White's visit, six years after Mr. Spalding came and of the Great Council and the laws he made for them. Mr. Deffenbaugh reads the laws and then asks, " Do you remember it all clearly ? "   " Yes, yes," they answer.

Jimmie Slickpoo's mother-in-law rises to tell about the Whitman massacre, and afterwards Isaac Wap-tas-kune tells all about the same thing. They were among the Cayuse Indians at the time. They gave the horrid details, which I do not wish to repeat. Will only say this. They both spoke of Joe Lewis as a Mormon.

These old people all say, "We had worship after Mr. Spalding went away." Luke, Jude, Joseph, Timothy, Levi and Eagle led them in their worship. Mr. Spalding was absent about twenty-four years.

So the five days of the Semi-Centennial went by in giving these little details. The evenings were what would now be called "popular meetings." A sermon by one of the natives—then the meeting was open to all, something like our prayer-meetings of the present day—prayer and song, mixed up with witness-bearing. Every once in a while through these evening services some old man or woman would rise up, and in thin, broken, tremulous tones, sing some very old hymn, that I had never heard before. Sometimes the one who had started the hymn would sing it entirely alone. Again, two or three voices would join in from the different parts of the congregation, plainly saying, "But few of us are now left to sing the old, old songs of Zion which Mr. Spalding taught us."

Mu-tu, Phœbe's mother, sang "The Prodigal Son" throughout. She had not forgotten a word of it.

The Story of Mu-tu

The name "Mu-tu" means "Down-the-river." Down-the-river, you exclaim. What a name! There are queerer names than that one here, and always will be, I think, for if the babe is given a Christian name when it is baptized, it is a kind of Sunday-best name. For home use it must have a long Indian name. Some of the names have some reason for them. For instance they call General Howard, whom they know and love, " Ah-tin-moot " (without-an-arm). The wife of one of their agents had gold filling in some of her front teeth, and was called " Golden Teeth."

But I must pass on—only touching the border of this great subject of Indian names, and come back to Mu-tu.

She came down to Lapwai a short time before the Semi-Centennial meetings in the new Lapwai church. Slowly she comprehended what was meant by celebrating the fiftieth anniversary of the Nez Perces mission, and concluded to remain until the meetings were over, for she could remember much about the first missionaries. It was amusing to listen to the talk among the people about what kind of a meeting a semi-centennial would be. They thought it so strange that the old people were especially invited.

I sewed two sheets together and filled it with straw to make a bed for Mu-tu in my house, while she stayed for the meetings. She told me that she was in Lewiston the day before, twelve or fifteen miles distant, and saw there such a nice, warm, red, woollen hood, and said, " I did want one for the winter so much. You know how far I have to ride to church in Kamiah. (Eight or ten miles.) But I could not get it, for I only had two bits (twenty-five cents)."

That afternoon she earned four bits more, piling wood, and as much more the next day. How rich she was then. One dollar and twenty-five cents! She put all her bits together in a kind of pocket with strings to it, and tied it around her waist under her dress, telling me with a beaming face, like a happy child, all she was going to get with that money. First of all, that hood, and then, tea, coffee and sugar for the winter. She would go to Lewiston for her things after the meetings were over.

The meetings began the next day, with Mu-tu always present—morning, afternoon, and evening. On the last day, Mr. Deffenbaugh explained to them what a thank-offering meant, and put the question, " Now is it in your hearts to make a thank-offering to the Lord for what He has done for you?" There was no response. He said, " If such is in your hearts, I will receive it, and send it to the Board of Foreign Missions, so they can send, or help send, the light to some other tribe, or people, sitting in darkness." One after another stepped up to the stand and laid down their silver pieces. Their silver " bits " must have turned to gold under the Master's eye, for none of them were rich. A few women slipped up, and among them Mu-tu.

Elder Billy sat with Abraham in the seat just before me. I could not help it. I whispered to Billy, " Won't you please find out how much Mu-tu gave?"

His son Robert at the stand received the offerings.

Without attracting attention he did what I requested and whispered back to me, " One dollar."

One dollar to the Lord, and twenty-five cents for herself !

I could see—not the dollar, but the coffee, the sugar and tea for the winter, and that beautiful hood—all lying at the Master's feet.

In a moment two pictures came before me. At first glance they seemed just alike. But, no. This Nez Perces widow, with her old shawl, faded dress and cotton handkerchief on her head, looked darker and older than the Jerusalem widow, but there sat the very same Jesus over against the Treasury, watching the gifts and turning, said, " She hath cast in more than they all."

XIII

FOURTH OF JULY CAMP-MEETINGS PAST
AND PRESENT

Struggle Leading to Separation of Christian From Heathen Camp—
The Separation—White Ministers—Heathen Parade—Miss Fraser's
Letter—Camp at Meadow Creek.

IT was strange that " King George's men " (Hudson
Bay Company) should tell the Nez Perces about the
Fourth of July, and that it was good to have a gay
time then. We have often wished they had taught
them something else, because out of this there has
come so much trouble.

During the time Mr. Spalding was away, from 1847
to 1871, they gathered to celebrate the Fourth, not
for one day, but for two weeks, by drinking, gambling,
horse-racing and getting new wives. Such a camp
this was in Kamiah when the Lord sent those Yakima
ministers to them with the message which brought the
old, wild doings to a sudden stop. From that time
on, for many years, the character of these July
assemblies was changed, for they were kept well in
hand by the sessions of the now well-organized
churches, within whose bounds they camped. The
sessions selected camping grounds, and were very

163

careful to choose a narrow place, fearing if they did otherwise, the temptation to race their horses on the long stretches would be too great for the weaker ones.

In those camps religious services were held, day and night. Some years each church would hold its own meetings. Then again the Kamiah people would visit the camp in Lapwai, and perhaps the next year the Lapwai people would return the visit, the churches in Meadow Creek and North Fork joining in the worship in either place.

In 1887, the agency had been removed—not permanently—up to the fort, four miles away from the Lapwai church. We then had a Boston lawyer as agent. He was in favour with the class of Indians who loved the races—and I presume he did also. About two weeks before the Fourth of July, he called on Mr. Deffenbaugh, who was then in charge of the mission, to see if he would not sanction the races, and give his consent to the Christian people camping with the heathen, on the grounds at the fort, close to their old race ground. There was no room for a race-track while the camp was kept near the church.

Of course, Mr. Deffenbaugh did not approve of the agent's plan. He told the people on Sabbath that he protested against the arrangement. But the week before the Fourth Mr. Deffenbaugh was called away on business and had to remain over the Sabbath. The native minister who was assisting Mr. Deffenbaugh announced from the pulpit that the people would pitch their tents up at the fort on Wednesday. There would be religious services each day and communion on Sabbath.

Mr. Deffenbaugh came home, perhaps the following Tuesday, and found the people preparing to go into camp. What could he do at this time? I told him what I would do. That I should not appear on the ground, for any, not even a religious service. Mr. Deffenbaugh felt that he must go and assist in the sacrament.

The Monday following was the Fourth, and such a Fourth they had not had since their heathenism. The agent rode at the head of the procession, which was spectacular enough to please him, and the more than two hundred whites from Lewiston and region round about, who stood watching the display from the verandas of the fort buildings, enjoying the sight, even to the naked men who helped to make up the procession.

The Fourth over, the races began. Delightfully situated! So thought the racers—and many in camp, for the Christians could sit in their tent doors and see all that was going on—just the creek between. Some of the more thoughtful Christians saw the danger to Christianity. Good old Elder Paul came to me and said, " I now see the door is open back to heathenism."

A part of the session grew more and more troubled each year, as they saw the life of the church slowly ebbing away in these July camps, and would come, and—Elijah-like—sit under the juniper tree (their own, not mine) saying, " The church is gone. We alone are left. What can we do ? "

That camp was the leak in the dike to let the flood of sin in upon them.

Mr. Deffenbaugh left the mission in 1888, and the native who succeeded him was not able to stem the current—so turned and went with it. He and his elders talked the situation over many times with me, and when I protested against the mixing-up of religion with the heathen doings of the camp, they would say, " We must follow the people to guard them from the sins there." How hard it was, and how long it took, for them to see that it was their place to step out and call the people to follow them. As the iniquity of the camp grew stronger each year, the church grew weaker and weaker.

The allotting of the Indian lands began in 1889, and Miss Alice Fletcher, the allotting agent, was in my house when the elders and Sunday-school superintendent came, with bowed hearts, to talk over another coming and much-dreaded Fourth of July—that of 1891. She heard their troubles and said, " The road is open to the good commissioner, Thomas J. Morgan, at Washington." This gave them better hearts. They would make their requests of him, asking that racing, gambling, and immoral practices be prohibited on the fort, or now government school, grounds. This petition they made ready.

The agency at this time had been moved back to the old place near the church, and there was a large training-school at the fort which closed its term the last of June. A few of the Kamiah people came down and hurried their children home, but most of the pupils, young men and maidens, left the school grounds for the camp, there to be dipped and dyed in the old heathenism. This, to me, was one of the most heart-sickening things about it.

My home was now in one of the old government buildings at the fort, four miles from the agency.

Not many days after the elders and Sunday-school superintendent had forwarded their petition to Washington, there was a council of the wild ones in the agent's office, to plan for their Fourth of July, appoint committees, etc. While they were in the midst of it, a telegram came from the commissioner to the agent, which read as follows : —

" You will see that my order to School Superintendent McConville to fence up the race ground and forbid all heathenism and immorality on school grounds is carried out."

What a stir that made, and how angry they were. Who had been writing to Washington? With one voice, they said, " Miss Kate, Miss Kate! " " The people will never have one heart while she is on the ground. How can we get her away ? "

My friends often said, in those wild days, " They will kill you. Do not sleep alone in your house. You are the only hindrance in the way of their returning to heathenism."

But I never left my house for one night.

That Fourth of July the camp was made just outside the school ground, half a mile away, and heathenism still raged.

Until 1893 they had religious services in the camps. Then they were given up, and with all restraint removed, and heathenism given free rein, war dancing, and so forth, went on night and day. They were always encouraged by surrounding white people. Renegade Indians from almost every tribe on the coast came, delighting to introduce new immoral plays into the Nez Perces camp. Oh! the vileness of it all!

When the reservation was thrown open, in 1895, and the Nez Perces began to receive payments from the government for surplus land, in order to get this money from the people, the white man added his vices to those they already had. Groups of Indians gambling by the roadside were a common sight. The slot machine was here, and every device that could be thought of, to get their dimes and dollars.

In 1893, Rev. Alexander Adair was sent by the Mission Board to Lapwai, and in 1895 there was a little band of Christians gathered in the camp near the church. Mr. Adair tried hard to rally the depressed followers, but the heathen camp near the fort attracted the crowd. This demoralizing camp continued each year until 1897, or for ten years after the flood-gates were opened, which not only nearly swamped the Lapwai church, but all the others felt the effect to some extent.

Where was I these ten years? Standing alone, until 1894, when two of the elders and a few Christians refused to go into camp. In the next two or three years, a few more were added to the opposing number, and in 1897 the elders said, " Let us have our own camp, even if there are only two or three of us." In the few years preceding, the churches had suffered great losses. Miss McBeth had died in 1893, Robert Williams, the faithful Kamiah pastor, and his father, our dear old Elder Billy, died in 1896. Death had called good Elder Paul from the Lapwai church. Three of its elders had resigned. Those remaining were Abraham Brooks, Matt Whitfield and John Allen. The Lord had been preparing these men for the hard work before them, and they shrank not from the fierce conflict when they saw it clearly their duty to help the Christians out of the deep mire into which they had fallen.

At the spring meeting of the presbytery in 1897 they showed their troubled hearts, and the white brethren there encouraged them to take their stand for the right. A letter was written to the Nez Perces Christians by Dr. Gunn, the Synodical Missionary, which closed with the text, " Wherefore come out from among them, and be ye separate, saith the Lord, and touch not the unclean thing, and I will receive

you.   And will be a Father unto you, and ye shall be
My sons and daughters, saith the Lord Almighty "
(2 Corinthians 6: 17, 18).

About two weeks before the people were to go into
camp, the elders called Rev. James Hayes, of the First
Church of Kamiah, down to Lapwai to read the letter
from the presbytery to the people, which he did after
preaching an appropriate sermon.   The announcement
was made that the Christians would camp in the government school field at the fort, which would leave
only twenty acres, the mission ground, between the
Christian and the heathen camp.   The session further
announced that they expected all Christians to pitch
their tents there, but if they chose to camp with the
heathen, they must stay there.   There was to be no
crossing over from one camp to the other—not even
to take the Lord's Supper, which was to be administered
on the Sabbath.   Those who went into the heathen
camp were to be considered suspended members until
such time as they chose to show sorrow for their acts
and confess their sin.

Some of the leaders of the wild ones were sitting
just inside the church door, listening to this, and there
was a great muttering among them.   As soon as the
service closed, one of them rode around the church,
giving in a loud voice an invitation to all Christians to
come to the heathen camp, and announcing that there
would be worship there.   He said, " No one has any
right to divide the people.   The Lord will do that

when He comes." And many a weak brother and sister felt as he did.

Sure enough, they tried to have worship, with George Waters, the Yakima minister, conducting the services.

Now the battle was on, and every one must show his or her colours. It was, " Who is on the Lord's side? Who ? "

You can imagine what a hard thing it was, for drawing the line so closely meant separating families, Christian from heathen, and almost parting husbands and wives. Indeed, some of our good Christian women were told by their heathen husbands, " If you do not come with us to the heathen camp, we will get other wives." And these were the fathers of their children, and so several women with very sorrowful hearts went into the heathen camp the first year. The question with us all was, who will be strong enough to stand this severe test ? The strife was so fierce it seemed as though it was a hand-to-hand conflict with the devil.

From that on, our hearts were up and down, for we often heard the report that this or that church on the reservation was not coming to our help. Nevertheless, at the appointed time our Lapwai committee pitched their tents and began preparations by hauling wood and tent-poles from the mountain, twenty miles away, for the expected visiting brethren.

The great worship tent was put up and nicely seated

and lighted with chairs and lamps from the government school.

Preparations were also going on in the heathen camp with great vigour.

Oh! what anxious days they were, and how we watched the people to see whether they would turn into the Christian camp or pass on to the other side. Our hearts were gladdened by seeing the bravery of some, and saddened by the weakness of others. How happy our Lapwai people were when they saw coming to the Christian camp Rev. James Hayes, with nearly all of his First Church of Kamiah, Rev. Moses Monteith, with many from the Second Church of Kamiah, Rev. Robert Parsons, and his Meadow Creek people, and Rev. William Wheeler with a number from the North Fork church!

The load was lifted from our hearts. It seemed as though we were living in Nehemiah's time and that these faithful servants had heard the sound of the trumpet at the weak point, and the cry, " Resort ye hither unto us. Our God shall fight for us!" Nobly, also, did the white ministers of the Walla Walla Presbytery rally around their Nez Perces brethren. How much we owe to them for always holding up our hands here.

The first white minister to arrive was a young man, lately from the East, who had taken up work on the Nez Perces prairie. The next was the oldest minister in the presbytery. They had a room in my home.

Those who came later lodged in the Rondthaler Cottage, the students' home near by.

Remember, our house was just between the two camps. On one side was the sound of tom-toms and war dancing. On the other, the songs of Zion and the praise of worshippers.

Fourth of July came. A great day among the heathen! They were to have a sham battle, and a parade, the horses to wear trimming and the riders to be bedecked in paint and feathers and to wear war bonnets and beads. It was to be a most gorgeous display—their recent payments making this possible. From my chamber window the old and the young minister looked over to see the stir, and the forming lines of warriors in the heathen camp. Going to the foot of the stairway a little later, I called up to them, but there was no answer. I then looked out the back door. Could I believe my eyes! Yes, there far in advance was the young Eastern minister making for the heathen camp, the older one following as best he could over the rocky creek bottom! Their presence of course gave the heathen great pleasure, and also furnished an excuse to our weaker ones for breaking over the line drawn and entering the heathen camp to gratify their inclinations as well.

The next day, Elder Matt Whitfield followed me out of the worship tent, with a troubled face, and said, " Miss Kate, we want you to make a ' *te-mas* ' (writing) for us to take to presbytery with charges against those white men for going over to the heathen camp. The presbytery made a law that there should be no crossing over, and you know what a fierce struggle we have had to make this separation, and now these white men have broken our arms, and opened the road for others to follow them." I saw how serious it was, but thought, " The Nez Perces will not be going to presbytery for more than six months. Perhaps they will forget it." But the next April, when on my way to presbytery, Elder Matt came running up from the church, and asked if I had that writing. I asked, " What writing?" He replied, " The charges to presbytery against those white ministers." I said, " That is not my business. That is yours. I only carry the session records." He said, " All right. Then Eddie (E. J. Connor) will write it for us."

He did, and Elder Matt carried the document, which was examined by the presbytery, and the offenders were severely reproved. Our elder came home quite well satisfied to think the presbytery did not pass lightly over the breaking of a law, although it had been made for Indians and broken by the white brethren. The offenders laughingly told the presbytery that I should be called up to make my bow, for if I had not given them the field-glass to see the heathen sights, they might never have been tempted to go.

The day of the Fourth we heard that the wild ones had planned to lead the heathen procession around and right through the Christian camp. This, the

Christians considered, would be an insult. They went to Col. Edward McConville in the school office, to tell their trouble, and he at once said, " Forbid them setting a foot on school grounds, and if you need any help, call on me." After a few minutes' hurried council, seven Christian men rode out and formed a line across the road on the edge of the school grounds in front of the mission home. They turned their horses' heads facing the oncoming hundreds. The lane was full, from fence to fence, for a quarter of a mile, with yelling, painted Indians. On they rode, till they came to the line of seven Christian men. They were determined to pass through, but were halted, and there were several speeches, first from one side—then from the other. The seven men never wavered. It was, " Thus far shalt thou go, and no farther." Finally the multitude turned their horses and rode back the other way, and we felt that the day of miracles was not yet past.

I did not see it all. I had fled to the One who was able to hold the glittering pistols in the belts.

We all felt, when that camp-meeting of 1897 was over, that although the church roll was not quite so long as before, those who took their stand on the Lord's side were strengthened by the separation. It seemed now to them they were no longer going with the current, but had faced about to stem it. How closely the Christians in that band seemed to be bound together now. We could see this in many ways.

Quite a number of church-members that first year camped with the wild ones, notwithstanding the strict law made by the session. Some of these disobedient ones did not make their appearance in church for weeks afterwards. How lonely they must have felt, after years of regular attendance! The churches are the centres of interest throughout the tribe. It is hard even for the godless to stay away.

Our eyes were anxiously scanning the people each day in search of the missing ones. One by one they slipped into their old seats, and as the next communion approached, the elders kindly, but firmly, reminded those who were in that camp of the law which had been made—that if they did go there and stayed there, they were to be considered suspended until they confessed their sin and sorrow for it. I see by the session book, that before communion day ten had appeared before the session, eight women and two men. The first woman to come said, " It was not with my own will I went to that camp, but all of my family went there. I did not feel good after I got there, and soon after went back to my own home." Another said, " I went with my daughter but stayed only one night—then crossed over with my bedding to the Christian camp."

The law was they were not to keep crossing back and forth.

One was an old woman, almost blind. She said, " I came from the Potlatch Creek—went with my children, not knowing there were two camps." Another took her seat saying, " It was not of my own will. It was my husband's will. I had no wish or desire to go, and after I was there I felt as if I were tied down with strong cords." All knew this good woman was telling the truth. The next had about the same story, saying, " My husband commanded me with power to go to the heathen camp, and said, ' If you do not go, I will take another wife there.' " The next woman said, " You know my husband, my mother, my brothers, all go to that camp. My husband said to me, ' We separate right now, if you do not accompany me.' " The last woman had the same excuse, " My husband commanded me to go."

So you see this line ran right through families. The Nez Perces are strong characters, and require heroic measures in dealing with them. All who came before the session with burdened hearts, confessing their sin, and promising not to go back again, were restored. Each one was asked, " Did you take any part in the heathen performances there ? " Not one had, although two of them acknowledged that they watched the others. A few, a very few, of the church-members who entered that camp, have never been restored. Only three, I think.

To belong to the session of an Indian church means hard work. From a human standpoint, if it had not been for the two strong men whom the Lord had but lately called to the eldership, and the Sunday school superintendent, this pulling of the church out from the heathenism into which it had been sliding for the last ten years could not have been accomplished. From that camp-meeting of 1897 to this day, the Lapwai church has been growing in strength. It is to the front now—a well-ordered, well-established church, with its Sabbath-school, its Christian Endeavour, and its missionary and temperance societies, which are models for the other churches. In its contributions it stands second in the presbytery. Is it not always so, when an individual or a church gives up compromising with the world and the devil? The Lord shows His approval and gives His blessing. The very next winter after the separation into two camps, the Lapwai church received such a blessing as it had not known for years.

How often I felt like saying, "Now let Thy servant depart in peace," for I have lived to see a band of Lapwai Christians strong enough to stand alone against heathenism.

Next year, the two camps were in just the same places—the mission ground separating them, the members of the Lapwai church nearly all in the right camp. But oh! what a blow we received from an unexpected quarter, for when the friends from Kamiah and Meadow Creek came stringing down to the Christian camp in great numbers, one of the native ministers, two elders, and some church-members from the Second Church of Kamiah, boldly passed the Christians and mission house, and entered the heathen camp, guided by one of their wild leaders of that camp. The music struck up over there giving them a hearty welcome. This minister was not in charge of any church at that time. Of course, they then had religious services in that camp. Even those men and women over there wanted the name of religion over them. We, in the Christian camp, could hear their war drums and dancing, while they could hear our songs of praise. Later those two weak elders resigned—it was the easiest thing they could do. The minister's case was taken to presbytery, and he was silenced for six months.

In that Christian camp that second year it was decided that the camp-meetings should be held after this, in or near the different churches. Lapwai was considered strong enough now either to be left at home, or to be a visiting church. A large tent was bought by the people, and ever since that the meetings have been going the rounds of the churches.

The next year the heathen camp divided in two, and has never since been united. One company celebrates up near the old fort—not on the school grounds, however,—the other down on the banks of the Clearwater. The spirit has gone out of their camps. If it were not for the whites, who flock around them to see their doings, they would be even weaker.

The government talks of civilizing Indians, but wants them to appear at great fairs in their old heathen toggery, and go through heathen performances, which is not very consistent.

Tired as we are some years, the Christian camp-meeting must be kept up as long as there is a demoralizing camp to go to. The children, the young people, and some of the older ones, must go somewhere, and if no wholesome place is provided, they will go to the other place.

Miss Julia Fraser gives the following description of the camp of 1904, in a letter to Mr. A. J. Ralston, of San Francisco:

Miss McBeth, Miss Crawford and I have just returned from the Nez Perces camp-meeting, and I never had such a wonderful experience. I never thought that anything in this world could be so marvellous.

We have six Indian churches, and this year the Meadow Creek church, which is about forty miles from Lapwai, entertained the camp-meeting. Tent-poles, pasture and wood are provided by the hostess church, while the people bring their own tents, bedding and food.

To avoid the dust we went a day in advance of the people, and were comfortably settled in Elder Johnson Boyd's house before the Lapwai people came. Fancy living in an Indian's house. Everything was as neat and clean and attractive as could be. Elder Boyd and his wife moved out, and lived over in a tent on the camp, and left everything for us to use. There were three good-sized rooms in the house, and two of them had been newly papered. They were carpeted and well furnished.

It was an inspiring sight the evening the Lapwai

people came over the hills to Meadow Creek. These Indians are very courteous and polite, and every little particular is carefully planned. When they camped for lunch, a spokesman was elected, who was one of the five riding at the head of the procession, and who responded to the greetings given by the head of the Meadow Creek delegation.

The Nez Perces are passionately fond of children ; their own, of course, but childhood in general appeals to them. Two little children rode with the leaders of the procession, one a little girl and the other a boy.

After the leaders came the two-horse carriages, twenty-four of them (and several more came the following days). Then the horsemen—such a great body as I could not count. Now, those people had been two days on the road. It was hot and dusty and quite late, and we knew they must be hungry, but there was no undue haste or hurry or rush. No one broke line, but each waited for their assigned place, and then in a great circle the tents were pitched, back of them the wagons drawn up, and then the horses were all driven off in a great bunch to a fine pasture, several miles off. They told me there were at least five hundred horses. I know I never saw such a number.

In the centre of the camp was the beautiful little church, and directly back of it was the great tent, where all the meetings were held. And those meetings ! How often I wished you were there. And the singing—it was inspiring. These dear people put themselves so into their worship, their singing, their speaking, their praying, that you catch their enthusiasm.

Many hymns are translated into Nez Perces, and these they sing without the organ. There is a weirdness and beauty about them which cannot be described. Then Miss Crawford has taught them English hymns, for which she always plays the organ. They love to sing, and they would gladly put in every minute between meetings (and none of the meetings are short) singing. I used to wonder at Miss Craw-ford's power of endurance, but one of the young men evidently voiced the sentiments of all when he told her " We can rest after camp-meeting, when we can-not learn new songs." They all love her devotedly, and she has wonderful influence. Miss McBeth told me that her sister, Miss Susan McBeth, had always said to teach the Indians to sing, and sing in their own language, and that she believed the Nez Perces had had the Gospel fairly sung into them.

I had expected to write to you of the meetings on Sabbath, especially the communion service of the Christian Endeavour and Sunday-school and temper-ance meetings, of the patriotic service on the fourth, and of the great feast on the fifth, when the Indians entertained over six hundred people at as elaborate a banquet as I ever attended ; but I really must leave something to talk about when I get home.

Miss McBeth does not need to go on the platform to reach the people. She will sit down on a wood-pile and talk (of course in Nez Perces) to a leader, and an hour later I will be thrilled by such a speech on temperance as I never in all my life heard. Of course it is in Nez Perces, and I don't understand a word, but I do get into the spirit of it.

This is the bright side of life here : the heathen camp at Lapwai, where gambling, racing, intemper-ance and all sorts of vileness go on, is the dark side. And yet white people flock to see it and to make money out of it. The lines are drawn very sharply between the heathen and Christian Indians, and necessarily so. There is a long story about this which I will leave for another time. But we can be greatly encouraged at what has been accomplished, and the success of the past must cheer us on to greater things in the future. But, oh ! I wish you were here to see it all !

Each year there are numbers leaving the heathen ranks to camp with the Christians. There were five Christian families in the camp at Lapwai in 1906 who had been heathen and pitched their tents with the war dancers the year before.

XIV

THE ALLOTMENT OF LAND

Miss Fletcher and Miss Gay—Opening of the Reservation—First Missionary Society—Presbytery—Rev. James Hayes—Synod at Moscow—What the Nez Perces are Doing for Themselves.

Miss Alice C. Fletcher, the allotting agent, reached the Nez Perces reservation in the summer of 1889. She came as an unpleasant surprise. We had heard indirectly, not officially, of her approach. Our agent at that time had failed to talk the allotting business over with the people. The Nez Perces are usually very cordial in their greeting of strangers, but there was no hand-shaking with this good woman. How ashamed some of them felt after they knew her, because they had received her so coldly. Many were opposed to allotment—not to just receiving their land in severalty, but to the giving up of the surplus land, and to the settlement of the whites among them, which they knew would follow the allotment. The next Sabbath after she came, she, with two other ladies, appeared in the Lapwai church. It was a sad looking assembly, the women especially giving but momentary glances at the strangers, and asking me on the outside, " Which one of these women is the one ? "

They had no spirit in the singing that day. Their harps were on the willows. There was depression in pulpit and pew. They could hear in the near future the tramp—tramp—tramp of the incoming whites on the home land, although the government about thirty years before had promised they should never be disturbed, if they would enter within reservation lines.

It is hard to make changes among the Indians, but Miss Fletcher knew how to deal with them. She met them in councils and patiently explained to them that it was the inevitable, and that time would show this move was for their good.

She did not stay long in Lapwai, but moved on to Kamiah and lived in the old mission house. There was not much opposition to the allotment among those of Kamiah, but their opposition was strong against the selling of the surplus land after the allotment was over. Miss Fletcher's kindness, with her business ability, soon endeared her to the class of Nez Perces anxious for Christian citizenship.

She allotted land to each of the then four organized Presbyterian churches, also to the Catholic mission, and showed an interest in their welfare. Through her, Mrs. Thaw of Pittsburg, became interested in the Nez Perces mission, and with her own funds she repaired the first Kamiah church, also helped the Meadow Creek church finish their building, and when the reserve was opened for settlement, Mrs. Thaw bought every acre of allotted church ground, at the government price, and had the patents made over to the Presbyterian Board of Missions. By so doing, she prevented any trouble in future about this land. It could not revert to the government after that.

More than this, she built the mission house at Lapwai, which has been such a comfort to the missionary for these now fourteen years. I might say it has been a comfort to the brother ministers in this region. Many of them have said, " We, too, thank Mrs. Thaw for this home."

Miss Fletcher and her friend Miss Jane Gay spent the summers of four years with us here. They not only strengthened the cause of right by their teaching, but by their example. There was no business done in Miss Fletcher's office on Sabbath day.

She tried to have the Indians choose the very best of the land. With all the people, the first question was, " Is there a good spring on that piece of ground?" She tried to get as many as possible from the Joseph band to come down from the Okanogan country and take up their allotments. Yellow Bull came down, and she fancied he would make a good farmer, and talked to him about it. He said, " I must have the Red Rock Spring." Miss Fletcher said, " The land there is poor. Let me show you where the land is good." He said, " No. I drank of that spring when I was a boy, and when sick and tossing in fever in Indian Territory (he was one of the Joseph captives) I drank of it in my dreams. Give me the Red Rock

Spring or I want nothing." She gave him that, with some good land besides. He is living beside that spring to-day.

It was necessary for her at times to call the tribe together for a council. I was with her once in such a multitude, and thought she richly deserved the congressman's pay which she received. She had a good surveyor with her, also a native who acted as her interpreter and driver.

We three had but one heart, this true friend to the Indian, Miss Fletcher, her companion, Miss Gay, and I. This was as it should be. She represented the government, and I the Church. Citizenship and Christianity should go hand in hand. Just here, I think, is the mistake the government has made in its school work—thinking only of citizenship. Citizenship without Christianity is but a veneering which time wears off.

How much company and comfort these two good women were to me.

When the allotment was over, Miss Fletcher had not much more than reached Washington before three commissioners appeared upon the ground, to buy the surplus, or unallotted land. There was much opposition to this. The most of the people thought it was all right to have their land in severalty, but wished to let the unallotted land be kept for future generations. They would say, "What are we going to do with our cattle and horses?"

After much hard work the commissioners got the

number of names required. Then, later, every once in a while, we heard the rumour, "The money is coming." But it was delayed so long that those who wanted it said, "It will never come." But they knew it was near when a company of soldiers from Walla Walla arrived—ordered to Lapwai for thirty days. They did not expect to need the soldiers for the Indians, but to keep in check the rough element which had been gathering in great numbers, at Lewiston, and at all points near the reservation.

This was in the fall of 1895. Late Saturday evening, three men, well armed, brought the checks from Lewiston. Monday morning the payments began.

Seven banks from towns near by were represented on the ground, each having a room in some agency building.

No one but Indians were allowed inside the yard, and just outside stood the guard of soldiers. They took the allotting list and read off a name, then a man would step to the door of the agent's office and call in that person, who was duly identified, and gave the required number of signatures. He then received his check, and by that time a representative of some of the banks at hand was ready to pay homage to the red man, for what he could get of his ready cash.

That was a time to test the honesty of the Nez Perces. Many of them had debts. I think, with few exceptions, they hunted up their creditors and paid them. Two Nez Perces came as straight to my house as they could, with the money in their pockets. One of them had owed me—perhaps for ten years. The other one had years before been sick, and of my own will I sent a physician to him. He now wished to pay for this. Of course, his money was not received. Honesty is a well-known trait among the Nez Perces tribe—so well known, that when anything is missing around a white man's ranch, he will say, " It was no Indian that took it."

What about the effect of these payments upon the people? The most of them made good use of the money. They built better houses and barns, and bought American horses and sewing-machines. A class—not a large class—of gamblers and drinkers went through their money just as fast as they could, and this class will doubtless sell their land when the twenty-five years are up, and then beg, I suppose, for the rest of their lives. Often I have wished they might have received their land without any payments, but to take their lands for nothing, of course, would not have been just.

Oh, such poor looking white people as passed up to take up land on the Nez Perces prairie ! I can hardly believe they are the same people who now pass down to the Lewiston Fair in the fall, in comfortable family carriages.

The Nez Perces prairie has brought forth by handfuls. It is said to be more fruitful than either the Walla Walla or Palouse country.

" Do the Indians work ? " Yes. We were afraid they would still cling to their valley homes. But, no. They are mixed up on the prairie with whites, and get along very well with their neighbours, even if they are considered " crazy on religion." They attend their own churches, which is well, and are often shocked by seeing the plow and reaper going in the white man's fields on Sabbath day, and by stores being open on the Sabbath. Elder Whitfield came near to blows a few summers ago, in trying to prevent the work of threshing on the Sabbath day on land he had leased to a white man. It was so with another man who was having a house built. Now they are wise, and put the clause into the covenant, or agreement, " No work on the Sabbath day."

As soon as they had money, repairs were begun on their churches. Each church was examined, and if the foundation was not good, work began there, and went on up to the belfry. They were newly papered or kalsomined, painted, inside and out, and a new roof, if needed, put on. Some of the churches got new organs. It was not hard to give for the needs of the church.

These payments were small to the individual, but because they came to the whole tribe at the same time, it seemed a great amount to the whites, as well as to the Indians.

Dear Miss Fletcher is still a comfort to us, even if it is more than fourteen years since she said good-bye.

I can see her yet shake her head, as she said, " Oh, no, I cannot come back to visit you, the people would all want their allotments changed at the first sight of my face." That unsettled feeling has passed away and I think all are satisfied with their new homes which are such an improvement over the little crowded houses or tents. It was hard for them to leave the graves in sight of the old home. They bury now around their churches. Let any trouble about a corner-stone or a line fence, spring up, then they come asking, " Is Miss Fletcher still in Washington? Won't you tell her this or that and ask her to go to the Office about it?" And how often she has helped us. We know her heart still beats true to the cause of the Indian, even if she has left the government service. Aside from her general interest in all the tribes, we love to think of her as a God-given friend to the Nez Perces Mission.

THE MISSIONARY SOCIETY

It required some tact and energy to start the Woman's Missionary Society. I invited a few of the advanced Christian women to spend the day with me, and cut out some warm undergarments for a few of the poorest of the old women, and while at the dinner table explained to them the workings of a missionary society. Such women as Mrs. Reuben, Mrs. Abraham Brooks, Mrs. Edward Reboin, Mrs. John Allen and Mrs. Timothy could understand quite well, but they were afraid of the talk it would make on the outside of the church. They said the men will make fun of the women officers. The next Sabbath after services in the church, the missionary had a little talk to the women there, inviting them to her house the next Thursday, prayer-meeting day. She closed her remarks with a quotation from Pastor Williams's address of years ago, when he was explaining to them about the first picnic—" Now if your heart is not with us in this matter, and you do not want to accompany us, be silent. Do not hinder others." The responding " Aah's " on every side showed the plan was approved.

Thursday afternoon brought twenty women. The society was organized,—not just according to the laws of the manual, for the missionary nominated all the officers. Mrs. Reuben was to be president, and her heart was sick at the thought of it. I told her I would always be near. The society was to be partly an aid society, for our church was poor,—so poor that it had never been properly seated. " Let us get seats for that middle block instead of those old school desks," said the leader. " Taats " (good) was audible. There was to be no membership fee, but a month from that time they were asked to bring a free-will offering, in money, or gloves, moccasins, Indian baskets, or whatever they could make that would be salable.

Their bashful fears had not been unfounded. At the next weekly prayer-meeting Mrs. Brooks and Mrs.

Reboin slipped back to tell me how one man was laughing at the " women bosses." I told them not to listen to what he said, that I had been expecting to hear from him. They went away comforted.

The first Thursday of February seemed wintry, and the snowflakes were gently falling—the first we had had. The meeting was to be just after dinner. Early in the morning I looked out of my kitchen window. Was not that Nancy? I might be mistaken in the pony, but never in that light buff sunshade with its deep border of lace protecting the new head handkerchief. She rode around to the back of the house to hitch her pony, with an air of, " I am not afraid of the men." Mrs. John Allen and another woman from Cottonwood arrived in the morning. Of course, these distant ones must have a cup of tea.

Phœbe and Janet, young Indian women from the school, came over and wrote their names in the big book. Each gave two bits. Soon Harriet came to write her name, and gave four bits. We sang while they were gathering. Mrs. Reuben, the president, got away off in one corner. I asked her to pray. Of course, she did. No Nez Perces woman ever refuses to do that—and before she knew it, she had opened the missionary meeting. We sang and read part of the twelfth chapter of Second Kings, the whole service being as much like a prayer-meeting as possible. The expectant look gave way. The room was full. Seats became scarce, so the woman in the red blanket from old Jacob's tent slid down to the floor, where she felt more at home. Old blind Jane, one of Mrs. Spalding's pupils in the forties, was given a rocking-chair. She was led there by another old woman. Helen appeared with her two babies. She preferred the floor. Every seat was filled.

When the time came for the offerings to be laid upon the stand, I had Mrs. Timothy, the treasurer, take a seat there. To my surprise, the quarters, half dollars and dimes were laid upon the table almost too fast for me to write the name and the amount, and I wondered how much would we feel that we could give, dressed as these women were !

A few pairs of gloves and moccasins were put down. I told the president and vice-presidents that they must decide what should be done with these articles. After a whispered consultation they said, " We want you to send them East and sell them, but not until we make more and bring them in next month."

Would you believe it ? Mrs. Timothy rolled up in her handkerchief, nine dollars in silver, besides the gloves.

Their work is not so very nice, for the wilder the woman, the better bead and fancy work she makes.

What a pleasant meeting we had ! They mounted their ponies and rode away with light hearts and beaming faces.

In three months, or three meetings after this, they

sent articles for sale to Washington, Pa., and their offerings in money have come to $15.60.

The June meeting was appointed for Cottonwood, ten miles away, in Elder Allen's house. We made a kind of picnic, taking our dinner along, but we did not refuse a cup of tea or coffee. As to conveyances? Oh! that is no trouble at all. I cannot think of a woman so poor as not to have her own pony to ride, though she may have but a home-made wooden saddle and plaited hair bridle for it.

Some of these dear women of the missionary society are very helpful to me. Mrs. Timothy or Mrs. Abraham has often gone with me to see the sick. Their voices in prayer are musical to my ears, as well as to those whom we visit. I hope all missionaries have just such women as some of these Nez Perces women are to help and cheer them.

Fourteen years have passed and still these faithful women love their missionary society. New seats were put into the church. The old desks thrown out. The seats the missionary society put in served until the payments for land came, when the whole church was remodelled. The women put in the last twenty dollars towards getting the bell, and did many other things to make the dear church look beautiful.

It is not all home work with them. Each year both the Home and Foreign Board are remembered.

Now the Lapwai women prefer to meet at the mission house. It is made to look just as bright and cheery for their eyes as possible—partly because few of them ever see inside another white person's house. There is always a cup of tea for those who come from away off eight or ten miles.

And now there are missionary societies in five other Nez Perces churches, so five of our churches are in line with our white sisters. This Lapwai Indian Woman's Missionary Society was for some years the only missionary society in the presbytery. It is like all other missionary societies—not all of the church-members belong to it.

Of late years I only read the Scripture lesson, and tell some little about other missionary work. Then the officers take the meeting in hand, which is always carried on with spirit. There is no hesitancy in leading either in singing or in prayer.

The Presbytery

What changes and growth we have seen in twenty-seven years! According to the statement of Dr. Gunn, for years our beloved synodical missionary, the presbytery of Idaho was organized at Walla Walla, Wash., in the spring of 1879, out of the state of Washington, Eastern Oregon, and the territory of Idaho, which area now covers the presbyteries of Spokane, Central Washington, Walla Walla, East Oregon, Kendall, and Wood River. That old large presbytery of Idaho was formed around the Nez Perces Mission as a nucleus.

WALLA WALLA PRESBYTERY AT KENDRICK, 1903

The Synod of the Columbia consisted of the presbyteries of Portland, Willamette, Southern Oregon, East Oregon, Idaho (as above), Puget Sound (including the presbytery of Olympia and of Alaska, then all in one presbytery).

I recall distinctly the picture of the Walla Walla presbytery, in several of its sessions. There were only three or four white ministers, looking all the whiter because of the dark Nez Perces background, as many as twelve or fourteen native ministers and elders, who usually came on their ponies no matter what condition the roads were in. How they did enjoy their first ride on a steamboat on the Snake River! We were going to Waitsburg to presbytery. Many pleasant remarks were made by the passengers as to their appearance and manners. One curious daughter of Eve came bustling up to me with the question, " Are you taking these men to Washington ? " It was the Waitsburg people who first opened their doors to entertain the Nez Perces at presbytery. They have received like honours ever since. Very happy were they to entertain this presbytery and their white brethren twice in their own churches, one year at Lapwai, and another at Kamiah, for hospitality is one of their graces.

Presbytery and going to presbytery were much talked about for years after the Nez Perces began to preach to their own people, and because the going and seeing were such an education to them, the missionary strengthened rather than weakened their desire. Often several more than the appointed delegates would ride out on their little Cayuse ponies into the great world beyond. They did not need to ask for a permit from the agent to go to this meeting, as for other journeys.

The happy party would carry the tent and provisions for not only the way, but for camping while there. It was no offense in those days if they were not taken into the homes of the church that was entertaining the presbytery, but now there is no difference, the Nez Perces are treated just as well as their white brethren. The Nez Perces were then so poor that Miss McBeth had much care and anxiety about their clothing to see that they were all presentable before the presbytery. The first ordained minister was hard to fit, and not at all particular about the looks of a garment, if it were only loose enough. A happy day it was in the little mission home, when on the eve of a meeting of presbytery a box of clothing arrived from some friends in Pittsburg, Pa. There was a coat just right for Robert Williams, and Miss McBeth gave it to him with the charge to keep it carefully for presbytery—the one he had would do for home service. But at that time the great heart of this man was full of other thoughts than clothes, for this was about the time of the breaking out of the Joseph war, and strange Nez Perces who did not wish to enlist under Joseph's banner, were slipping within the reservation lines.

Among the number who came into the Kamiah community was a mother with her three boys, from the fierce White Bird band, Joseph's helpers. One of the three sons, a large-framed boy with long hair, paint and blanket, soon followed the Christians to the church, but was too timid to go in, and the first Sabbath stood around listening to the sermon from the outside. The next Sabbath he slipped into a seat near the door. The Spirit fastened the truth which he heard from Robert's lips so that he was anxious to hear more about the new way, and his conversion soon followed. His flowing locks were cut, the paint was washed off, his blanket laid aside. He was dressed in the precious presbytery suit and Robert led him to Miss McBeth in triumph.

As soon as she could speak to Robert alone she said, " Oh! Robert! why did you give away your presbytery coat? You know I am anxious to have you respectably clad among the white ministers." He was surprised to find her so vexed, and said, " Miss McBeth, he is a Christian now, and wants to begin to study with you; he could not come in a blanket and had no coat. I had two coats, and the Bible says, ' Him that hath two coats let him impart to him that hath none.' " The boy took his place in her schoolroom and what comfort she had in watching both mind and heart develop under her training, and how strong the tie between him and the pastor, Robert, till death separated.

That big overgrown Indian boy in Robert's presbytery coat was our beloved James Hayes, who is now
a man of great influence not only among his own people, but a chosen vessel to carry the gospel to the
Shoshones and many other tribes.

Synod at Moscow, Idaho, October, 1896

I doubt if ever a happier company left their homes
for an outing, than did more than thirty Nez Perces
men and women who started out on the first day of
October last for the synod of Washington, to meet
that evening in Moscow, twenty-eight miles distant.

Rev. D. O. Ghormley's invitation to native ministers, elders and students was closed with " Brethren,
bring your wives along; we will provide for your
camp." The women often make trips with their
husbands to the mountains, driving the pack ponies
before them, but had never dreamed of seeing a presbytery—much less a synod. Not one wished to be
excused. Many of the company reached the Clearwater Ferry before the sun was up. The steep mountain grade on the other side was tedious, but no one
was impatient. We met many a surprised traveller
that beautiful day. One understood, for he explained,
" They are Presbyterian Indians, going over to that
meeting in Moscow."

When we reached the suburbs of the university town
a halt was called, and the driver of the hack with the
missionary in it, was told to pass on and take the lead.

Such a procession of spring wagons did not pass through the streets unobserved. They were soon comfortable in camp, and presented themselves at the first session of the synod, and throughout the meetings were usually in attendance, even though some of them could scarcely understand a word. There they met eastern and western friends of mine of whom they had often heard. They had a part in the exercises, and sang often in their own tongue. I knew that their fine appearance would be remarked, for Nez Perces men are larger than other Indians of this coast. I had often to say, " Oh! but we have plenty of blanket Indians at home."

We reached home on the evening of the fifth day, without an unpleasant occurrence to brood over, but with tender memories of sacred scenes, where Christians looked into each other's faces, sat together at His table, and felt that we were all children of the same Father, travelling towards the same home.

What the Nez Perces are Doing for Themselves

There are about five hundred Christian Indians in our Nez Perces churches. What are the Indians doing for themselves? The six churches are supplied with native pastors and led and governed by native sessions. Their decision in judicial cases sometimes seems severe to white people, but they know their own people and how to deal with them in the best way. Some of the most difficult things in church government are taken up to the annual camp-meeting, where all the native ministers and elders are assembled, and, in a solemn and most dignified manner, the matter is discussed. One of our white ministers led the class in church government last year, and was greatly perplexed at some of the questions that were asked, and finally had to say : " Brethren, we have no such cases in our white sessions, and I cannot decide for you."

Even if these white brethren are puzzled over some of our problems, they are much help and comfort to us. We see much of them, for they are always interested in the work here, and for two successive springs the Walla Walla presbytery has met in Nez Perces churches and been entertained in Nez Perces homes.

As many of the white brethren as can do so come to our annual camp-meetings, and sometimes there are ten or twelve present at a time, to give help and encouragement to the Nez Perces, and are just as often helped themselves by sitting down among our devout worshipping people, as they witness their zeal and earnestness. If all presbyteries within whose bounds the Indian missions are established, would be as helpful as our Walla Walla presbytery, how the work would be lightened for the missionaries !

What are the Indians doing for themselves ? From an outside standpoint the answer would be, they are self-supporting. Their little houses on their allotments are most of them quite comfortable. True, they are still receiving some help from the Board of Home

Missions, but, for several years, two of our churches contributed to the board almost as much as they received from it.   Last year Lapwai came next to Walla Walla, second in the presbytery in its contributions, just as Kamiah had stood several years next to Moscow.   I have never favoured their separation from the board, even although they contributed as much as received.

As to the mission class.   Little, or very little help is given to them.   These men move back to their farms in the spring and work through the summer for the next winter's needs.   My most advanced pupil took his team and went for weeks with a threshing-machine, hauled wheat, etc., thus adding to his winter's store.   In this way their schooling is rather slow, but character is strengthened by it.

XV

MISSIONARY EXTENSION

Neighbouring Tribes—Visit from a Bannock and Shoshone—Rev. James Hayes at General Assembly in Philadelphia, Pa.—Shivwit Indians—Letter from Rev. Charles M. Kilpatrick—First Marriage and Baptism Among the Shivwits—Rev. Mark Arthur.

WHILE Mr. Spalding was with the Nez Perces he often took his helpers, a class of students, and went out to preach the Gospel to neighbouring tribes. Rev. G. L. Deffenbaugh did the same in later years, and, as a result, two churches were organized among the Spokanes and one among the Umatillas. Those pulpits have at times been supplied by Nez Perces ministers. After the white ministers had left the Nez Perces field, the natives took up this work, going in a different direction. Rev. Robert Williams, a Nez Perces, with his little company of native Christian helpers, went for several years in the summer season over among the Shoshones at Lemhi, intending to go farther south to the tribes there. But in 1896 the Lord called him up higher. Then, Rev. James Hayes, a native also, who succeeded him as pastor of the First Church of Kamiah, continued to carry on this mission work.

In 1897 he and his helpers pushed on farther south to the Shoshones near Fort Hall. The people there

REV. JAMES HAYES, WIFE AND TWO CHILDREN

The Young Man Standing Is James Dickson

showed no interest, neglecting even the common Indian hospitality of giving them food, or inviting them to their homes. Again they went the next year, but not until the third year was there any change in their bearing towards the Nez Perces. Then they began to see that the Spirit was quickening the seed. Five men came and said they wanted to give up the old way and be taught of the new, and baptized. James, with his usual caution, told them to wait until he returned a year later. Then, if they were still of the same mind, he would baptize them.

When he was about to start home they brought to him a Bannock boy of about seventeen years, and said, "Take this our boy home with you and keep him close by your side. Do not let him go to Lapwai." (Lapwai was considered a wilder part of the tribe.) "He can see how you worship God and come back and tell us." I heard of the young fellow being in Kamiah. One day, about three weeks after my school began in Lapwai, James came in with the Bannock boy, and said, "Miss Kate, although they told me to keep this boy at my side in Kamiah, and not to let him come among the wild ones in Lapwai, I find I cannot do it. I remember, years ago when Miss McBeth talked to Robert Williams as he was about to start on his missionary journeys, she would say, 'Try to bring a boy home with you for the school, so that he can be taught of God, and then go back and teach his people.' I know this boy should be taught, and everywhere I go I hear Miss McBeth's voice speaking to me, just as she used to speak to Robert. Even when I was on the mountain after my wood, and everywhere, I heard her voice. Now here he is. I cannot keep him any longer."

The boy found a home with one of my student's family, and studied with my class of men.

At Christmas time the Nez Perces always pitch their tents about the church for their communion season. That year they were surprised to have a Bannock and a Shoshone enter their camp.

The very day those two strangers arrived in the camp at Lapwai, I had sent down an invitation for the session to meet the three new trustees at my home the next day, up at Fort Lapwai, as my place is often called. We had never had trustees before. It was a new thing. The elders had always managed temporal as well as spiritual affairs, and did not now seem willing to hand over any of their authority. The matter must be talked over in the presence of all. My dinner was well on the way when the first delegation arrived and told me at once of the two strangers who had reached the camp the night before, and that they, also, were coming up with the rest. But what was I to do? My table was set for seven. I had just so many knives and forks. However, the two young trustees, E. J. Conner and Elias Pond, smilingly tied on the aprons offered them, accepting the position of waiters upon the table with a good grace.

After dinner, the difficulties were not so hard to arrange. The strangers knelt with us while we asked wisdom and guidance, in temporal as well as in spiritual affairs. At the right moment, I, as church treasurer, handed over to the trustees the eighty dollars which they should have had long before. These difficulties were settled for all time so far as the session and trustees were concerned.

I watched these officers and the two strange Indians ride away from my home that day, with the feeling that this visit was but a repetition in substance of the visit of the four Nez Perces to St. Louis in search of the truth. The Bannock was over six feet tall, with his heavy braids falling on his breast. Overcoat on, however. Except for that he might have passed for a typical Indian of fifty years ago. Pat-ty-hee was his name. He acted as interpreter, having some knowledge of the language obtained through one of his old wives, who was a Nez Perces. The other stranger, the Shoshone, was Alex Watson, a pleasant, citizen-looking man, anxious to receive just the same kind of religion the Nez Perces had.

They said, " We could not wait till that boy would come, to know how to worship God. Neither could we wait till the snows melted from the intervening mountains. So we sold a spring wagon and some pigs, and came quick by the cars."

After they went home, they wrote back, saying, " We are not very wise, and do not know whether we

have it right or not, but we have two services on Sabbath and one during the week, and are trying to worship just as the Nez Perces do." Miss Amelia J.
Frost, who had worked so faithfully for those Indians
while under the Woman's Indian Association, was
transferred to the Presbyterian Board of Home Missions,
and has most efficiently and lovingly cared for this
church since its organization.

The missionary spirit among the Nez Perces was
strengthened by a visit from Miss Axtell, of Lake
Forest, Ill., in 1888. The two friends, Miss McBeth
and Miss Axtell, planned for the going out each summer of some of the Nez Perces to other tribes, Miss
Axtell and her two sisters, Mrs. Pratt, of Denver, Col.,
and Mrs. Rumsey, of Lake Forest, furnishing the
means needed for these journeys. True, the Nez
Perces went on their own ponies over the mountains,
but in such a journey one man needed as many as
three ponies, for they must change off and so rest them.
The shoeing of so many horses for the mountain roads
was quite an expense. It was not two or three
who formed the missionary party, but a dozen
or more. They must have their singers along and
cooks, also. In those years, when they went out
they carried with them Gospel sign cards, with
some Bible truth in the sign language, as well
as words, upon them, so that even the older men
and women in the tribes to whom they might go
could have a share of the Gospel feast. These cards

were prepared by Miss Axtell, with much care and at great expense.

How the sisters there in Lake Forest and the sisters here followed the missionaries in their yearly journeys to Southern Idaho ! James Hayes tells of them in the address which he gave before the Woman's Board, in Philadelphia, during the General Assembly. He said, " My friends, although it is about other people I wish to talk, I must tell you a little about myself, first. I was a wild heathen boy when the Joseph war began. I was one of the White Bird band. According to the custom of olden time, the boys were sent to the mountains to live days and nights alone until some animal or bird would come and speak to them. Then we trusted in its spirit to protect us after that. A long time after I came to Kamiah, I could not see the light, Then, through the preaching of my red brother, Robert Williams, my blind eyes began to open. He took the blanket off my shoulders, put a coat on me— cut off my hair—then led me to Miss McBeth's school, where I began to study the Bible. My friends, you know the rest about me.

" Five years ago some of the Christians of Kamiah went with me on a missionary trip to the Shoshones, on the Lemhi reserve, where there are both Sho-shones and Bannocks. It was a rough road over the mountains. In one of the deep canyons, we killed a bear. I think we travelled, going and coming, 600 miles that time five years ago. We stayed at Lemhi about a week. The Indians did not want to hear about Jesus there. Not many came to our meetings. I made up my mind we would go further, to another reserve, Fort Hall. So the next day in the morning I showed my heart to my companions, telling them some of us would go and some wait until we return from Fort Hall. Next morning we took a ride to the depot. So we went on the train at eight o'clock in the evening and came to Ross's Fork at two o'clock in the morning. My friends said, ' What shall we do ? Where shall we go ? ' I said, ' Let us go to the creek and stay in the bushes.' At eight o'clock we came out from the bushes. Then the Indians met us and asked us, ' Where did you come from ? And what did you come for ? ' I told them, ' We came here to tell you about your Saviour, Jesus Christ, and about your souls.' The Indians went back to their homes. They did not listen to us any more. Only one man took us to his house. We stayed with him one day and one night. Some of my companions went to Pocatello, and stayed all night. Myself and two brothers went to a Shoshone tent. We were there a whole day and night without any food. My two friends had sorrowful hearts. I took out my Bible and read to them the eighth chapter of Matthew, the twentieth verse, ' Jesus said to them, the foxes have holes and the birds of the air have nests, but the Son of Man hath not where to lay His head.' After these words we had prayer. Next morning we left that reserve and went back to Lemhi, and from there home. Next year I finished my mind to go back to Fort Hall reserve. That time Brother Lowrie Sibbet was with us.

"Dear friends, it is hard to say how many miles we travelled over the desert land. It might be eighty or ninety, without any water for ourselves or our horses. That second time, when we went back to Fort Hall, just a few Indians came to our services to listen to what we preached to them. But the third time, many Indians came and asked us, 'What is religion? And what do you do?' I explained to them. Then five men promised to try to be Christians. I told them, 'If it is God's will, I will come back next year. I will not baptize you now. Then, if your heart is still open towards God, I will.' They could not wait a whole year to know more. In the winter two men, a Bannock and a Shoshone, were sent to the Nez Perces land to see how we worshipped God. They stayed with us three weeks, visiting with us in our churches. The fourth time I went, I was appointed by the presbytery to go and stay six months. I went with my family and one of my elders, and organized a church of eighteen members. At this time the Christian members are seventy-two. Also a church building is now finished. I think two hundred people can worship in it.

"Now, my friends, I have a little story to tell you about the Shivwit Indians of Utah. Last fall I took a trip away down into Utah. When I came to Salt

Lake City, I thought, ' I am a stranger in this city.'
But after that I found Rev. Mr. Paden of the First
Church of Salt Lake City, who was kind and helped
me much. I was in that city four days. From there
I went to St. George, Utah, where the Shivwits live.
I was with them five days. We had services every
evening. The Indians attended well. I asked them
how many wanted to be Presbyterian Christian mem-
bers. They answered me by holding up the hand.
Fourteen persons. I hear many more now want to be
Christians. Long time ago they were baptized by the
Mormons. One thing more, dear friends, the Shivwit
Indians are very, very poor. I never saw people so
poor before. They need cloth. They need bread.
They need the Gospel of Christ. Remember them in
your prayers. What God has done for us, He can do
for them."

Miss McBeth died believing the Lord's word would
not return to Him void, but accomplish all she had
hoped and prayed for. Miss Axtell was permitted to
see the seed just beginning to spring out of the
heathen hearts of a few Shoshones. If the Church has
now special angels watching over it, looking down
lovingly upon it, surely Miss McBeth and Miss Axtell
know and rejoice over souls born into the kingdom of
God through the ministry of the Nez Perces. And
was it not lovely ! When the Fort Hall church among
the Shoshones was finished, Mrs. Rumsey, in behalf of
herself and her departed sisters, Mrs. Pratt and Miss

Axtell, sent the pulpit, pulpit chairs and Bible for that church, and will do the same for the prospective church among the Shivwits of Utah. This is a most glorious progression. Shoshones first, Shivwits next, and this year the call comes for James Hayes to cross over into Nevada.

The call to come over and help us in Utah, came from Miss Work, who is the government teacher and agent, also among the Shivwit Indians, and Rev. Charles Kilpatrick, a white minister living at St. George, near them. It was a long journey for James, being about 200 miles beyond Salt Lake—a part of the way by stage. He could not pass unvisited his dear Shoshone friends, even although he had seen them in the summer—so spent a Sabbath going and one coming in the Fort Hall church, and on one of these Sabbaths, administered the Lord's Supper there. His visits among them often remind me of Paul's to the churches of Asia, so strong and tender is the tie which binds their hearts together.

James reached Shem, Utah, the last week in November. He had been there a short time a few years ago, so the Indians met him as an old friend. The meetings began at once. It did not take some of them long to finish their minds, or to decide to throw away the old heathen ways and follow Christ in the new, and a few soon asked to be baptized.

James cautiously answered, " Not just yet," for he wished to consult Dr. Wishard, synodical missionary, who soon came and advised an organization. A little later James wrote to me, saying, " To-day, nine persons confessed their faith in Jesus Christ." Two days later he wrote, " The Christians now number sixteen, and we expect two more to-night." When he came home he brought the good tidings of twenty-eight having declared for Christ. These are the first Christians in that heathen tribe. It was evident that the Lord's spirit had been preparing the ground for the seed. We, here, would have been greatly disappointed if it had been otherwise, for prayers went up daily from these Nez Perces homes for God's blessing upon James and the people to whom he had gone. A letter received from Rev. Kilpatrick may be interesting here. It reads as follows:

Mr. Hayes came to St. George, as you doubtless know, November 27th, and assisted Dr. Wishard with the communion service Sabbath morning among the white people. It was a very precious service, although there were only eight of us present. Then he preached for us—to whites, Sabbath evening. The house was crowded and many were not able to get in, all anxious to hear an Indian preacher. Monday Mr. Foster took him up to the reservation where he held two services each day for ten days. I was obliged, very much against my will, to be away most of the time, but spent the last three days with him. Mrs. Foster is an old mission worker here, and she told me she had never attended meetings where the Spirit was so manifestly present. The Indians quite generally laid aside everything else, and as far as they were able attended all the meetings. The results have greatly shamed my own weak faith. I have hoped for, and expected to see an Indian church here, but I had not dared to hope that more than three or four of our Indians would be ready at this time to take a definite stand and pledge themselves to live for Christ, but when, in spite of careful and heart-searching examinations, twenty-eight of them, most of them heads of families, took a firm and definite stand, I had no more spirit left in me. When Mr. Hayes told us that after his visit here three years ago his people gave an offering of forty dollars to help build a church for our Shivwit Indians, I said, " Oh! Lord, give me such faith." We have all, both Indians and workers, been greatly blessed and cheered by his visit, and he also greatly endeared himself to us all by his cheery, genial ways. We especially enjoyed the stories of old Indian folk-lore which he told us. We hope to build a church soon on the reservation if the Lord will open the way for us, and I believe He will.

James baptized twenty-eight adults and six children. He married a couple—the first Christian marriage in the tribe. Among the church-members there are several from other tribes or bands who are scattered through the surrounding country. We hope these may prove to be light-bearers to their own needy people. Fortunately, they can all understand the Shivwit language. James thinks these people are not so wedded to old customs as some other tribes, but if temptations are not so strong from that quarter, they will have the demoralizing influence of Mormonism among and around them. The Mormons worked among them years ago. Then threw them away—

perhaps because they were so poor. Brighter days in temporal as well as spiritual things are dawning upon them. Houses are going up, and I understand the government offers a certain amount of lumber to each man who will build a home for himself. What a step forward that will be—from a little bark structure, partly underground, to a new board house.

Mr. Foster, the missionary there, and his wife, James loves very much, and thinks they will take the best of care of that little band of sheep in the wilderness. Although Miss Work has moved from them, yet, being agent, she will often visit and have a watch-care over them.

We are happy to state that the church among the Shivwits as well as the one among the Shoshones, is growing. The Nez Perces have raised a sum for the new Shivwit church at Shem, Utah; also that for the present at least, the amount needed for the expenses of our evangelist has been assured, largely through a good woman in Geneva, N. Y.

This year, 1905, James Hayes and Mr. Kilpatrick pushed one hundred and twenty-five miles beyond the Shivwits up into the mountains to the Kaibab government boarding-school at Panquitch. Seven of the boys and girls gave their hearts to Christ. Not a single adult of this tribe is at this writing a Christian. From Northern to Southern Idaho, and beyond five hundred miles into Utah, we can see the beacon lights shine out in the darkness. This year a call for the gospel comes from the Moappa Indians of Nevada, two hundred miles farther on. We see in warp and woof the golden thread of God's love running through this web of Indian progression. We see also the Hand which guided Speaking Eagle and his friends into St. Louis, seventy-five years ago, is still guiding His own work here. Our sainted Mrs. Pierson had a glimpse of this Gospel-lighted way, when she wrote:

"And so from Nez Perces to Bannock and Shoshones, from Bannocks and Shoshones to Utah and Nevada tribes, the Gospel progression lights up the dark corners of the country, while the dusky torchbearers show to a lagging church how the light might be turned on, were its own response as prompt and earnest."

XVI

DEATH OF MISS S. L. McBETH

MISS S. L. McBETH arrived at Lapwai Agency on the Nez Perces reserve in the fall of 1873. Although an employee of the government, her appointment came to her through Dr. Lowrie, secretary of the Board of Foreign Missions, for at that time the educational work on many of the reservations was largely under the control of the different denominations.

Dr. Lowrie was no stranger to her; he had been her correspondent while she was a missionary among the Choctaws, and indeed, her coming among the Nez Perces had been suggested by her former associate at the Good Water mission station in Indian Territory, Rev. George Ainsley, who in 1873 was in charge of the little government school at the Lapwai Agency. Miss McBeth was never at any time a strong woman, and at the time of her starting West for her work among the Nez Perces, it was feared she had not strength enough for the journey. Little did her friends then think she would spend nearly twenty years of faithful service for the Master in that field.

Mr. Spalding at the time of her arrival, in 1873, was in Kamiah, where the presbytery had decided he should live, much against his own wishes. Rev. Cowley, now of Spokane, was also then in Kamiah in a little government school.

In 1874 Mr. Spalding was brought down sick to his beloved Lapwai, and died in a little government house within the school enclosure, which Miss McBeth called home. She always spoke of Mr. Spalding as a faithful missionary, a strong man. She had little patience with weak ones. She taught one year in the government school at Lapwai. Then, by advice of the good agent, John Monteith, she removed to Kamiah, and took up the work laid down by Mr. Spalding, which was the training or instructing of a class of five men for the ministry. Three of that class are now in their graves. Although as perfectly isolated in Kamiah then as if she had been in Africa, she ever spoke of her first years there with pleasure. There with intellectual relish she added daily to her dictionary and grammar. And when in the evenings her weak eyes were too tired to read or write, she would in her darkened room mentally translate the songs of Zion, dear to herself, into the Nez Perces tongue. From the first, Elder Billy Williams was her trusted friend, her almost daily visitor, and through him more than all others she became rich in Indian lore.

Her Kamiah schoolroom was a picture. There around this little woman sat not only her class of divinity students, but pastor and elders, with an occasional visitor as well, while the principles of Christianity and civilization were explained to them in their own tongue. If doubts were expressed, the leaves of the Bible were turned until the " Thus saith the Lord " was found, settling the matter with them forever. There was no unsound theology taught under the Kamiah pines. Was this little Scotch woman able for such work? Can any one who has read her " Seed Scattered Broadcast" doubt her ability to teach theology?

What effect has it had upon the church whose session sat as pupils in her schoolroom? All the ministers and students for the ministry came from that one church with but two exceptions. It is to-day a well-trained missionary church, sending out yearly evangelists to other tribes. The native pastor needs intelligent helpers. She knew that the only lasting civilization for Indians must come through the Gospel. Questions of law and order were discussed there, for Christianity and civilization among them cannot be separated.

She had enemies, as all strong characters must have. Hers were of a class. One of the chiefs once said to her, " You have been trying to kill the chiefs ever since you came on this reserve." She did not deny that she was trying to destroy their power over the people, believing as she did that no real progress could be made until the tribal relations should be broken up, and the Indian man feel his individuality, and not merely regard himself as a part of a band.

Miss McBeth seldom appeared among the people, but from out that schoolroom, through her pupils, went a strong influence for good, not only to every part of the Nez Perces tribe, but to the Umatillas, Spokanes and Shoshones as well. Often in reviewing her work would she exclaim, " Thank the Lord for Robert Williams ! I could have accomplished little without him." Like herself, he knew no fear of man.

She needed all her courage to stay up and strengthen the little hearts around her. For Indians are timid braves. Her strong will and her ability to read their hearts was ever a mystery to them. Under her gaze they felt they were being sifted and weighed. She was always upon the lookout for good material for the Lord's work. Some of these fine-looking men before us now, dropped their blankets and washed off the paint to enter her schoolroom. All hail the power of Jesus' name !

The schoolroom was but a part of her work; with Paul she could say, " Besides all this comes upon me the daily care of all the churches." Figuratively, she was always walking round the walls of Zion, marking her bulwarks, pointing out to the little band of native workmen the weak places to be strengthened.

At the breaking out of the Joseph war in 1877, she, with some whites, was guarded by forty-five loyal Kamiahans from Kamiah down to Lapwai, making the trip, sixty miles, in one day, in a farm wagon. This was no new experience to her. Christian Choctaws had guarded her out of the Indian Territory when Texas ruffians were more to be dreaded than the White Bird band. Her answer then to the call to come home was, " I am immortal until my work is done." She did not return to Kamiah until 1879. Her school for the time was kept up in Lapwai, but the most of her twenty years were spent with the Kamiah people, either in the Kamiah Valley or in Mount Idaho, which was at that time their trading town. She saw about as much of the people there as when living down beside the little church. How happy she was when her pupils with their families were comfortably housed for the winter in the cottages built for them at Mount Idaho. Did anything trouble their hearts while they were down in Kamiah, the little pony soon bore them up the trail to Mount Idaho to the " mother."

Sacred scenes must often come before these men now. No journey was ever undertaken, not even from Kamiah to Lapwai, or Mount Idaho to Kamiah, without kneeling beside this mother to ask the Father's care. Little notes came back to her if detained, and then as soon as possible after their return they reported to her. How they trusted her ! " Why," one of them said as we gathered around her for the last time in the Kamiah church, "she never deceived us once ! Let us keep her teaching in our hearts and follow close after her." But it was in her schoolroom the last winter of her life that this strong bond between teacher and taught, mother and sons, was seen. How anxiously they would scan her face each morning as she stepped with swollen feet from the sitting-room to the schoolroom! *For she must be there.* In a moment one of these gentlemanly pupils was at her side to help her to the chair, which another would place where she loved to sit. With her far-reaching eye and fast-failing strength she was fortifying them against the skepticism which they would meet in the near future. They must not be taken unawares. She never grew weary of the Lord's work. Often did she say in that last winter, " If I were able and younger, I would like nothing better than to go into a wild tribe and do over again the work I have done here."

At her own request, her body lies beside the little church she loved so well in Kamiah—beautiful Kamiah with its Scottish Sabbath. Need I say more about her work when you have here the living epistles before you? Full as her work among the Nez Perces seems to be, 'tis but a part—a small part—of the service this woman of faith and prayer was enabled to accomplish. The secret of it all lay in her early consecration to the Master and a consciousness that she was working, not for time, but for eternity. While teaching in Fairfield University, Iowa, now Parson's College, she was urged to give herself to literature. She gave her answer in a little poem, which I now give to you :

" Write a book, my sister !
     I am writing it day by day,
And the characters traced in that writing
     Can never pass from the scroll away,
For the parchment is a part of the Infinite,
     The soul is the vellum given,
By which with the pen of my life I write
     A record for hell or heaven.

" Oh ! a fearful gift is this author's life,
     For the lowliest guides a pen
Of words and deeds that leaves
     Its trace on the hearts of men,
And carelessly often the record is made
     And lightly we pass the thought
That we must account for the ill we have penned
     And the good we have written not.

" Oh ! not 'mid the planets which shine, my sister,
     In the galaxy of fame,
That is bounded by changing time, dear sister,
     I sigh to rank my name.
For the dust of earth is upon the stars,
     And the brightness will pass away,
When eternity ushers in the light
     Of that sinless clime of day.

" Oh ! then may my writing be approved
     By the searching eye of Him
In whose visible presence the sun shall fade
     And the glory of earth grow dim.
May He write my name in the Book of Life,
     With the dear ones He has given,
And I crave no other share, dear sister,
     In the fame of earth or heaven."

Miss McBeth was born on the banks of the Doon, in Scotland, and was buried on the banks of the Clearwater, in Idaho. The intervening sixty years were marked at every step by the guiding hand of the Lord, whom she so faithfully tried to serve even from childhood.

When but a child she read everything within her reach. There was not so much to reach after then! How she did love to have the children of the neighbourhood sit spellbound, listening to her stories from the " Arabian Nights," " Scottish Chiefs," and other books. If she ran out of stories, she drew upon her own imagination. At times she would challenge us to make poetry about some common object in sight. Notwithstanding all our efforts, we would fail. Then we would listen to her smoothly-flowing rhymes, feeling that she belonged to a higher order of beings. It was a loving act to her Master to take the talents which He had given her, and consecrate them all to His own service, instead of leaving them to her own guidance.

She met many serious obstacles in early life, but looked upon them, as she ever did in after years, as something for her to bend her energies to remove. She took great pleasure in watching them vanish.

While teaching in the Fairfield University, Iowa, she was called to go as a missionary among the Choctaws of Indian Territory. She was at Good Water station in that tribe, from 1859 to 1861, when she, with other missionaries, was compelled to leave the mission on account of the war. Nominally, the Indians were on the side of the South—probably because of their slaves. She returned to Fairfield University, but soon afterwards went among the sick and dying soldiers in Jefferson barracks and in the hospitals of St. Louis. She was the first woman, I believe, to wear the badge of the Christian Commission. She was there some time before she was commissioned. At the same time there was a young physician, with his wife, in the barracks, whom she often met. This doctor called her one day into their room, and with some embarrassment said he wished to talk to her just as if she were his own sister. He said that in the work she had taken up, he feared she would subject herself to remarks, as she was the only woman doing such work, and young, and that all the ministers and laymen working as Christian commissioners had commission from headquarters. She said, " Just give me your Bible, and I will show you my commission." He turned, the blood mounting to his brow, and said to his embarrassed little wife, " Have we a Bible, dear ? " Her honest answer was, " No." Miss McBeth went to her little room, threw herself down on her hospital cot, and had a good cry. In the midst of her weeping, she arose with a start, saying, " Sue McBeth, is it possible that you will allow a man without a Bible to hurt your feelings ! " " That is enough of this weakness." It was not long after this that she wore the badge as the other commissioners did. I rather think from the many, many letters she received from returned soldiers or their friends, that this part of her life was the richest in results of it all.

In removing obstacles from the way of a soul seeking Christ, and in presenting the plan of salvation in its beautiful simplicity, she had few—if any—superiors. While in the hospital work, she wrote many little tracts for the soldiers, which were blessed then. These tracts were afterwards gathered together and published in England, under the title of " Seed Scattered Broadcast." It was classed at the time with the Headley Vicar's Series, and commended as a text-book to all engaged in like work, whether in war or peace.

After the war, she became city missionary in Dr. James Brooks' church, in St. Louis. While in this work she helped to establish a home for the friendless young women of the city. A lifelong friendship existed between this city missionary and Dr. Brooks. They had one heart on the subject of the second coming of Christ.

Her next call was to the Nez Perces, where she spent almost twenty years. The last eight years of her life were passed in the little village of Mount Idaho, with her pupils around her during the winter, and resting in the summer months in that beautiful spot, with kind white friends near her. I went up every summer, going by stage from Lewiston to Mount Idaho, seventy-five miles, in one day. I said to myself, on my return trip in '92, " I think I shall travel this road again before the year is out ; " the dear sister seemed so different. Although in her usual health, she seemed to have dropped all care and anxiety about the mission. I was not surprised to get a note from her friend, Mrs. Wallace Scott, on New Year's day, " We think you ought to come up." I went at once. I found her busy with quite a large class, not the least alarmed about herself. She was too busy to think of herself. I was with her the most of the time until that bright morning, May 26, 1893, when she entered into the joys of her Lord.

She had spent such a full, busy life, memories of her childhood had been almost crowded out. They seemed so far away, but during that last winter she would often try to remember the name of this girl, or that boy, who had started out in life with her, or who used to be in the old home church. Now, while waiting on this side for the messenger, was the only leisure time she had ever known.

Brave she had always been. I recall an expression made but a few days before she died. She feared we thought she was shrinking from the last enemy. With her keen eyes, she looked at us, saying, " I am not afraid of death. I am not even afraid of the devil. He cannot hurt me."

She had her house in order, her will made. Robert Williams, the pastor at Kamiah, was to get her home in Mount Idaho, in remembrance of his faithful work as her helper among the people.   Her dictionary and grammar were to go to the Smithsonian Institute at Washington.   The last clause of the will, after mentioning the monument and fence for her grave, was that whatever was left of her money was to go to the board, to send her pupils to wilder tribes with the Gospel.   We see the blessing flowing from this now, for the missionary work of the Rev. James Hayes is partly supported by this fund.   She is still living among the Nez Perces, and has settled difficulties in session work even since her death, by some one of the session saying, " Miss McBeth said so-and-so in a similar case."

Precious work was hers, and glad I am that her mantle has fallen upon me,—even me, so much inferior to her, both spiritually and intellectually.

Her suffering was so great, I would not, could not, wish to keep her one day longer.   I was with her until she died.   According to her wish, we buried her just back of the little Kamiah church she loved so well.   Two white women and two drivers went with me down to Kamiah.   We reached the ferry at sunset Saturday evening, and were met there by a company of sorrowing Nez Perces, who came one by one, gave me a hand, and passed on—in silence.   We crossed the river and found another company awaiting us at her old home.   We at once placed her body on the platform of the pulpit, where it remained through the tender, touching services of the Sabbath, for she had taught them not to bury on the Sabbath. To the right of the pulpit sat her pupils with bowed heads and tears running down their dark faces—the younger ones sorrowing most. Sobs were even heard, when the oft repeated expression fell on their ears that Sabbath, " The Mother has gone. We are orphans now." Robert Williams tried hard to turn their loss to a blessing by urging all to follow her teachings, and praying for her same spirit of devotion to the Master. There were no cold services that day, and to the white friends with me it was most touching.

Although it was raining hard, and the hour for her interment early, seven o'clock Monday morning, the little church was again filled for the funeral services.

How proud the Kamiah people are to have her resting there! How sacred and beautiful the spot is. Kamiah is dearer to me than ever.

The dictionary of 15,000 words and grammar which Miss McBeth directed should be sent to the Smithsonian Institution was not all copied at the time. I took it with me from Mount Idaho—then myself placed it in the express office in Lewiston. I had written to the Smithsonian Institute about it. The answer was, " Send it right on. We think we can finish it here." Some correspondence was then in progress about my going East for a visit. It had been fourteen years since I had seen my old home. I left Lapwai Saturday morning for Lewiston, to spend the Sabbath there, so as not to be on the road the next

Sabbath. I took the precious box of manuscript. Gave it over to the expressman with many charges, for my sister prized it above all earthly things. No wonder! She had spent so many years here in carefully preparing it.

The question was put to me in Lewiston by many, was I going by boat or stage? In other words, was I going by way of the Union Pacific, or the Northern Pacific? This I could not answer, until Saturday evening, when the post-office clerk brought over a letter from the board in New York. Upon opening it, I found my application for half-fare ticket was granted by way of the Northern Pacific, which settled the matter. So at four o'clock Monday morning I was sitting in the stage bound for Uniontown. We had to wait for the Clearwater ferryman to come over for us. While waiting, the ill-fated *Annie Faxon* shot out from her landing, headed down the Snake River, not far from us. That boat was to make connection at Riparia with the Union Pacific Railroad. I can see it yet as it looked in the gray dawn. When we got out at Uniontown, I examined the boxes on the platform for the dictionary. " Where was it to go?" asked the man. " To Washington, D. C." He said, " Oh! it would go by the Union Pacific." Then I knew that we had parted company.

The next day the newsboy was selling papers in the cars. I bought one. The first paragraph I saw was, " The *Annie Faxon* blown to pieces. Boat a total wreck. All on board killed or injured." You may imagine I had food for thought that day. Wrecked fifty miles below Lewiston! Goodness and mercy have followed me all the days of my life.

But that precious box! With twenty years' work upon it! I wrote back to Lewiston from Butte City, asking if the box was on the wrecked boat. In due time the answer reached me in Ohio, " Yes," but they hoped it was not much injured. *Why?*

All the time I had lived at Fort Lapwai the clerk in the sutler's store there, with his young wife, had been on the best of terms with me. Two years before he had bought a farm on the Snake River, but moved to it only last spring. He understands and talks Nez Perces quite well. His home was some miles below where the boat was blown up. That morning he was on the shore of the river and saw much stuff floating down. His eye was caught by a red box. He mounted his horse and waded out as far as he could. He had a long rope tied to the saddle. He made a noose upon it—threw it out just as the red box was going over some rapids, and caught it. He drew it to shore, opened it, and recognized the Nez Perces script. He said at once, " This must be Miss Kate's sister's writing." He found it soaking wet—stood the paper up on the beach so as to dry, then went up the river some miles and found the cause of the drift. Saw the dead and wounded.

Mr. King, who rescued the box, was the only man I knew on either side of the river, from source to mouth. He returned, took all the manuscript as carefully as he could to his own home, where he and his wife placed it to dry in the loft. Next day an express agent from Portland arrived in search of this valuable box. Mr. King did not wish to give it up until the sheets were dry, but the agent said he had been sent for it and must take it. They would dry it carefully in Portland. In the meantime, I had written to the secretary of the Smithsonian Institution that the manuscript was on the wrecked boat. While still in the East, I received a note from him saying, " We have just received the dictionary. Cannot yet tell how much it is injured."

Dear old Elder Billy said, when I told him of this, " It seems as if that box were a living thing, and that the Lord was caring for it." The author of the manuscript had so many tokens of the Father's care while passing through this world, that this last act was but in keeping with the past.

XVII

JONATHAN WILLIAMS

First Orchard in Kamiah—His Work in the Sabbath-School—His Love for White People—Map of Nez Perces Land—His Death—Mission School at Lapwai—Mark Arthur.

LAWYER was the first elder in the First Kamiah Church. Billy Williams and Solomon Whitman were ordained soon after, by Mr. Spalding.

Jonathan Williams, better known as Elder Billy Williams or Ku-ku-loo-ya, was a small man, quick in his step, brisk in all his movements, and so genial in manner that the whites as well as his own people loved and welcomed him. Miss S. L. McBeth had written so often about him to the Foreign Board that one of its members called him " Miss McBeth's red jewel."

He was a trusted friend, with whom we could sit down and talk over anything that pertained to the good of the mission. His judgment was always good, even down to old age.

The first time I saw him he had on a dark blue coat made out of a blanket. He made it himself, he said. There was no spread out blanket on him after the Lord met him over in that camp-meeting in Kamiah.

ELDER BILLY WILLIAMS

The Historian of the Nez Perces Tribe

He it was, you will remember, to whom Mr. Spalding talked about garden-making, over in the house at the foot of Thunder Hill, when Mr. Spalding pared a potato, and handed him a piece raw, which Billy tasted and pronounced " taats " (good). The next year his garden was talked about everywhere.

His garden in Kamiah was always a source of income. He would take his vegetables over to the mines, where he was paid the highest price in gold dust. He knew how to charge, all right, and was so shrewd he got the name of " Business Billy " from the miners. He might have received the name from another source, for he often said in talking, " Much business me Billy." He wanted the same price for anything he had to sell near at home as he did away off at the mines. He did not count the time or trouble in taking the things there.

He had the first orchard in Kamiah. Felix Corbett the second. He was always busy. Had a shop near his dwelling, and there he made many useful things. It was a sight to see the many tools for work hanging on the walls of that shop, or on its shelves.

He was always clean and neat, but it was in church and in church work he appeared the best. For nearly twenty years he was sexton for the church, without pay. He looked upon any work about the Lord's house as an honour, and he did keep it nice, with the brooms hung up back of the door. He had the fires made and the bell rung always on time. He had his presbytery suit just the same as the students in the mission school.

He was a very acceptable teacher for the little boys. He knew his lesson quite well before he went to Sabbath-school.

Not long after I moved to Lapwai, Billy presented himself at my door, and before he entered he explained the reason for his visit. Carefully unfolding a tiny book which he had wrapped in a large head-handkerchief, and showing it to me with its fifty-two Bible pictures—one for each Sabbath in the year—he said, " I came down to have you tell me the story about each picture." I said, " I will tell them to you, but it must be mornings and evenings, for my school must go on." (He had come sixty miles for this.) So he came from day to day, and when going to his lodging-place in the evenings, he would often start away with, " I will think it all over in the night, and if I do not clearly understand, you will tell it over, won't you?" He loved, Isaac-like, to walk in the field and meditate. Then he would come to me with some such question as, " Don't you think David was married to Solomon's mother, but not to Absalom's mother, and that that is the reason there was such a difference in those men?"

If Billy was not the first man to have an allotment of land given him, he was very nearly the first. Billy had sensible views concerning the selling of the unallotted land. Many were opposed to it. They would say, "Shall we kill our horses? We will have no pasture for them. Then think of the hordes of whites that will flock in upon us." They were even then camping in great numbers on the borders of the reservation, waiting for the moment to come when they could take up the much coveted land.

Billy's main reason for selling the land was his pity for the poor old people, who were very likely to die hungry if the commissioners were refused the land. He knew as well as I did, that many had already died without comforts for the body. However, the commissioners had hard work to obtain barely enough names giving consent to the opening of the reservation to the government. The people of Kamiah especially opposed it. They were not opposed to the allotment of land, but to the sale of that unallotted.

Billy, with all his kindness and gentleness, was no coward. He was bearer of dispatches for Colonel Steptoe in the Yakima war, and was proud of telling of his exploits, when he was "*expressman.*" That was his word for it.

After the Joseph war the people of Mount Idaho were much enraged against the Indians, and although those at Kamiah had refused to join the Joseph band, still they were Indians, and of the same tribe. One man in Mount Idaho who had suffered much from the Joseph band said he would shoot the first Indian he saw upon the streets. The people there had been accustomed to getting their melons, tomatoes and such vegetables, from the Kamiah Valley, but there could be no intercourse while this bitter feeling lasted. Billy was sent for. Not knowing for what reason, he went. One of the prominent citizens of the town drew Billy's arm within his own, and paraded the streets. Of course, no one would hurt Billy. So friendly intercourse was again resumed.

He loved the whites, and was very much like them. How he did love to go to presbytery! He would have much to tell about what he saw there and on the way. Then he would try to have things as he saw them there. His first call upon me after being away at the presbytery once was made wearing gloves and carrying a cane.

He said to me, " I noticed this, Miss Kate, when I was away. It was only the wild whites who called us Indians. The Christians called us Nez Perces."

How tender his conscience was! On one of the missionary trips to the Spokanes with Mr. Deffenbaugh and native helpers, they were very hungry when one of them shot some kind of a bird or fowl. When at dinner it was passed to Billy, he silently refused it. There was no laughing about it. They knew that his " Wy-ya-kin," or attending spirit, was of the same species. Although he did not trust it now, he could not eat it.

Before Miss Fletcher went away for the last time, she sent up to Kamiah for him to come down. She wanted to get some Indian lore from him. He was rich in this.   She considered him the most reliable authority, or the best historian, in the tribe.   He came. He found out she was trying to see where the Indians came from, and from what direction they came here. Billy brightened up, saying, " I do hope Miss Fletcher will find me Billy an Israelite."   He was an Israelite indeed, without guile.

He would come over to me early in the morning, saying, " I could not sleep.   I was all night with those old people."   He was recalling olden times, and could not sleep.

He made a large map of the Nez Perces land, with its streams and seventy-five villages, naming each one. This was sent with his photograph and a short sketch of his life, to the Peabody Museum at Cambridge, Mass.

One day Miss Fletcher asked him to sing one of the old heathen worship songs.   He was a good singer.   At once his lips were set and a change came over his face.   He said, " I love Miss Fletcher, but I cannot do that without hurt to my own soul.   I have thrown all these things away long ago, and I cannot sing one line of the old heathen worship song."

Billy lived his long life with but one wife, the wife of his youth.   The only wife even in his heathenism —so that his large family were full brothers and sisters.   This was an unusual instance.

How much comfort he was, to both my sister and myself.   Often have I seen my sister so tired she did not feel as though she could say a word more, but when Billy came to the door, it was, " Oh! is it you, Billy! Come in."

The last years of his life I had a lounge for him to sleep upon in my house when he came to Lapwai. Billy was the only Nez Perces favoured in this way. We would go into the living room after breakfast or supper, and I would ask, " Where do you want me to read?" Without a moment's hesitancy he would say, " Mr. Spalding or Miss McBeth told me something about ———— but I did not clearly understand it. Please read there." He did not remember about the chapters, but would tell me something about the subject. While it was being read, in the Nez Perces, I could hear the approving " Aah!"

He led the prayer, in his own tongue—a prayer that led my soul into the presence of the Lord.

Although he was seventy-five years old when he died, he was just as bright and happy, his step just as elastic the last time he was down—about two months before he died—as it was many years ago. On his death-bed he had his son-in-law write, saying, " Tell Miss Kate, now I am going home, and the friendship existing between the whites and myself I bequeath to my family. Tell them this." He passed into the heavenly inheritance in April, 1896, not quite three years after my sister, and just ten days before his son, Robert, the pastor of the First Kamiah Church.

Sometimes even now, after over ten years have gone by, I get lonesome to see this good old man.

Many said, when this heavy bereavement came upon the First Church of Kamiah, " That church will be weak now." But, no! The workers fall, but the work goes on.

A word about the mission school, or class, for it is but a class. At the time of my sister's death in '93 there were a number of her pupils who wished to pursue their studies. I spent the next winter with them, in Mount Idaho. For several years after that they were at a standstill, so far as their studies were concerned. There was no place for them to live in, in Lapwai—only in a tent, which I was not willing for them to do, after living in houses for years. But the Lord who knows just when to act put it into the hearts of the ladies of the Tabernacle Church, of Indianapolis, to write asking me to tell them how they could show their love for their pastor's wife, Amelia Rondthaler, who had just passed from them. They knew her love for the Nez Perces—so wanted the memorial here. I saw the hand of the Lord in this, and told them of the need of a cottage here for the use—especially then, of some Kamiah pupils who had small families. When we had talked this over a little more, the cottage went up fast. It was ready for these Kamiah families that fall.

A great comfort that building has been to me ever since. It was built in 1896. It is near to the Thaw cottage, my home, and my pupils can be seated around my study table by eight o'clock in the morning. The wives are under the care of my niece. A delightful work is mine, opening the door into the treasure house by teaching my pupils how to translate the Bible. A pupil reads a portion, first in English. Then, while the others sit watching and listening, he cautiously picks his way, not pronouncing one word after another as in English, but following about the same rules a Latin scholar would in translating Cæsar, his teacher helping him at times over the hard places. When they find some precious truth, how their faces shine. Perhaps some one will remark, " We found an unfailing spring there."

We use the English for all studies but the Bible. I could not be sure that they understood the truth until they could translate it into their own language.

Friday is our Sabbath-school lesson day, also catechism and church government. Catechism is hard for them, but no harder than it was for us years ago. All the Sabbath-school teachers of the church school, superintendent and pastor are likely to be found sitting at my table on Friday morning. Sometimes some others. The elders come quite often to listen. Frequently we ask an elder, " Where would you like to have us read and explain to-day ? "

We shall feel lonesome without Elder Abraham this winter. He came oftener than any of the rest. He is now with the Great Teacher. His last words were to his wife, " I am ready now. Ring the bell." Likely he thought he was in the church he loved so well, for he always rang the bell. Abraham did not confine himself to the lesson in hand. One time it was, "Why is it that there are so many denominations among you whites? You have the same Bible, in the same language." Another time, he asked, "What is the root of politics? I know what the root of religion is, but these democrats and 'publicans, I don't understand."

The new songs are nearly always sung in my school-room, and happy they are any day to have me say, "Now you may sing a little while." (My niece at the organ.) One evening in the week, the families come into my home. There is first a little lecture. Then they sing.

The government training school is near to the mission house. There are always some very companionable people among the employees, but our greatest pleasure has been to lead the weekly prayer-meetings there among the children.

XVIII

NEZ PERCES CHURCHES AND MINISTERS

The Churches—Evangelistic Services—Letter Written by Miss Mazie Crawford—Reverent Nez Perces—Nez Perces Hymns—Ministers.

THERE are six Nez Perces churches at this writing. Since the land has been allotted the people are more scattered, many of them living up on the prairie, mixed up with the whites in everything else but in their religion. The Nez Perces want their own churches, with their own native pastors and elders. This is well for them spiritually. There is no need now for a superintendent of missions, in the sense that term used to be applied to the white minister whose home was always here in Lapwai. For years, it was but a nominal office. Good men and wise men they were, but it would take any one of them years to get the language so that they could preach in it. Indeed each one since Mr. Spalding's time has used an interpreter.

The great advantage a native minister has over the white man is, he can readily know what is going on among the people. Can see the wolf coming and give the alarm. A conservative white minister does not see the danger in Christians indulging in some of the old ways, and they have even said, " I see no harm in that." For instance, the Feast for the Dead, when all

244

the goods of the departed one are given away. Some of the white ministers have looked upon it as a kind of harmless, memorial service. The native minister understands the danger in this gathering of leading them back into the old heathenism.

The native sessions are amenable now directly to the presbytery, and if anything irregular occurs among them, they can be reported to that body. They certainly know how to manage their own churches better than any white minister can do it for them. They ought to have a missionary among them, to consult with, and appeal to, even if, at times, that teacher should be compelled to say, when certain cases of discipline come up, " You must be a law unto yourselves. No such cases ever come up before a session in a church of white people." Then there must be kept up a class, or mission school, where helpers for the native pastors should be trained. A native pastor, without intelligent helpers, will soon become discouraged. It was the mission school at Kamiah in the early days that made that church such a power for good. We see the mission school has had the same effect upon the church here in Lapwai, since its transfer to this place.

Our ministers have not the liberal education of the white men and have not been away to school. Some of the older ones have never been even in the government school. Rev. John P. Williamson, of the Sioux, said in a late article, " I am often asked, ' What educa-

tion do you give your Indian preachers ? Or what
sort of workers do they make ?' As few of these
preachers ever saw the inside of a college, I sometimes
answer, ' The same as the apostles. Three years or
more in indoctrination into the word of God,' and to
the second question, I answer, ' They have saved souls
to show for their ministry.' " Of course our younger
men have had better advantages, and will have increasing
opportunities for growth—perhaps by going East to a
Bible school for a term. We will try to keep abreast
with the times, not forgetting, however, the faithful
services of some of the older ones in the ministry.

As to the elders, we have had at times men in this
office wholly unfitted for the work. On the other
hand, we have had, have now, some elders who for
godliness and faithfulness to their trust have no superiors in white churches. They are present during every
service of the church,—at the Sabbath-school and
Christian Endeavour, the same as at the prayer-meeting. In sickness and sorrow among the members, they
are there found—perhaps holding an all-night service
of hymns and prayer in the house of mourning.
They often bury the dead if the pastor is away. It is
not light work to be an elder here. The sessions of
our several churches often meet and talk over the in-
terests of the kingdom—and plan for evangelistic
work within their own bounds. How the Christians
enjoy worshipping together. Often one minister will
send a note to another, saying, " Come and help us.

Bring some of your elders and people with you. We will look at a description of one of these meetings, given by my niece, Miss Mazie Crawford.

In January, 1903, the First Church of Kamiah held special services the first week in the new year. Rev. James Hayes sent down an invitation for our Lapwai pastor and elders, and as many of the people as cared to come, to spend Sabbath with them. When we met at the Lapwai depot there were twenty-one of us. We left at 3:15 P. M., arriving at Kamiah at 9:30. It was raining, and oh, so dark ! But James and other friends were there with five hacks, and we were soon off for the two-mile ride. There was a lantern on each dashboard, and we made quite a showy procession. When we reached the ferry across the Clearwater river, the boat was waiting. As it could only carry two teams at once and ours was behind, we sat there, waiting and watching the figures of the ferrymen as they moved about in the light of their lanterns, or the dancing reflection on the moving waters. When about mid-stream, James Hayes started a Nez Perces hymn, and the company with him, and those still on the bank, joined in. It just sounded beautiful, floating back and forth across the stream. The visitors were assigned their places among the Kamiah people who were camped about the church, but not all in tents. A number of them were, but the rest have built little houses on the church ground for use just at such times, for several live from ten to eighteen miles away from the " Temple," as dear old Elder Solomon calls the church.

The night service was such a warm one, we did not get home until eleven o'clock. Sabbath we were in the church just about all day. They had the Lord's Supper in the morning, Sunday-school at 2 P. M., followed by Christian Endeavour, and that gave us just time to get our supper and be back to the church for the English song service which always preceded the regular meetings. That night it was twelve o'clock when we were dismissed. I imagine you want to ask if they did not get tired. No, they never think of such a thing. I have known them to stay up, preaching, praying, and singing, until three or four in the morning. Their whole hearts are in it, and they would be ashamed to get tired worshipping God.

There was a closing service Monday morning, and the people then scattered to their homes. Tuesday morning's train brought us back to Lapwai. In all the services Rev. James Hayes was assisted by our pastor, Rev. Mark Arthur, and Rev. Robert Parsons, pastor of the Meadow Creek Church.

I had a nice time in the Indian home. Mr. and Mrs. Luke Williams are such a thrifty couple, and live just like white people, and were kind to me. I much enjoyed the family worship in their home. No difference how late it was, and how tired they were, it was never omitted. Luke, as head of the household, always took charge, but never took any more part than the rest of us. His sister and family were there, and we would sing and then one of the five Christian people would read the Scriptures, and another one lead in prayer. It was just so with grace at the table, too. Each gave thanks. But do not think we went around with long faces, for we laughed, and joked, and had the best kind of a time. Yet there was a quiet dignity about the home which kept the merriment from becoming too common.

We are to have special services here at Lapwai the first of February. We expect our Kamiah friends to visit us at that time and of course James Hayes will be here to preach some of his good gospel sermons, and in his loving, tender way plead for the wandering ones to seek the Lord before it is too late. He has such love for the people, and they give him such love and respect in return.

The Nez Perces have great reverence for the Church. This was well impressed upon some of our presbyters at one of our Fourth of July camp-meetings near the church at Lapwai in 1895. We, with four white ministers and several friends, had taken our dinner, intending to eat under the trees near the church. We had spread it out on some boards on the ground, when a very heavy rain began to fall. We were not long in deciding to go into the church. Two or three of the white ministers picked up the board on which our feast was spread. This procession was headed by one of the ladies carrying the steaming coffee pot followed by the remainder of the company laden with baskets, etc. They proceeded to carry the decision into effect. Two old Indian women sat under a tree near to the door and when I came up a few steps behind the others one of them exclaimed, " Miss Kate, why do you allow those whites to desecrate the house of God by going in there to eat ? " When I told the brethren how they felt, they meekly laid down the board, as if seeking protection from the rain only. It was a hungry party that stood there for an hour, waiting for the storm to cease, but not one mouthful did we dare to touch, for there sat the old women, eyeing every move, nor did they leave until we and our provisions were well upon the outside.

I have never yet seen any one, in any of the churches, turn around to see who was coming in, or whisper during church services. The church is the centre of interest in each community. It is the place to go to, even if some of the wild ones do not go inside.

It is a beautiful sight, on Sabbath morning, as we reach the top of Thunder Hill here in Lapwai, to look this way and that and see the ponies with their riders descending the steep hillsides, and count the spring wagons emerging from the canyons. It is said from every hamlet in England there is a road to London. So it is here. All trails converge at the churches, suggesting to me a picture of the Jews going up to Jerusalem to their feasts.

SOME HYMNS IN NEZ PERCES

GOD LOVED THE WORLD OF SINNERS LOST

> God hinashatwishana
> Pipaatokeshwishna,
> Shapukeshwit hinatse
> Nishana uyikalana.

CHORUS

> God-nim tsitsiwaish
> Hatawit,
> Panahpaik Saviourna.
> Inimwatsati hitinktsana.

Wako mitsekuinakitki,
Yoh witalahtoken,
God-nim Miyats hiwash,
Inim shapukeshwiyawat.—Cho.

THE LORD IS MY SHEPHERD

1. Lord hewash inim suptiumkawat,
   In watu hiyahnu,
   Ipnim sapatamaliku ina
   Yos-yospa tsik-tsikpa.

2. Ipnim hetelkakiku ina
   Kots-allie.
   Inim wakaswit heleulimkanu
   Ipnimki wanekitki.

3. Sekounie ipskekiku
   Tinkinim poholpa,
   Im ah wiatwatsam ina ;
   Inim Jakin sapahipstuenash.

4. Ekuin taatswit wah misheyoukt,
   Tewiktatasha ina ;
   In touyaneku Lordnim Init
   Kunku wah kunku.

THE LORD'S PRAYER

1. Nunim Pisht Aishniwashpa imim wanikt hautnin Kam watu.
2. Imim miohatoit ki anashapautsasham, Imim Kutki anashapautsam uyikashliph Ka Kush aishniwashpa, hikutanih.

3. Taks lahaipa hipt natsnim taksain.
4. Nuna wasatiai nashwaunim Ka Kush nun titokana wasatiai awaunaitanih.
5. Wat mat anashtahinawiyukum nuna, matu taklai nuna
   shapakapshishwiatupkinih natsnahwuinukum : Imin
   awam inakanikt, imim awam Kapskapsnawit imim
   awam siskeiwit Kunku.   Amen.

———

Rev. Archie Lawyer was pastor of the Second
Kamiah Church at the time of his death in the spring
of 1893.

Rev. Robert Williams, the first ordained minister,
ordained in 1879, was pastor of the First Church of
Kamiah at the time of his death in 1896.   This was
his only charge.

The Nez Perces ministers now living are :

Rev. James Hines, honourably retired because of
old age.

Rev. Mark Arthur, pastor of the Lapwai Church.

Rev. Peter Lindsley, without charge.

Rev. James Hayes, pastor of the First Church of
Kamiah.

Rev. Moses Monteith, pastor of the Second Church
of Kamiah.

Rev. Robert Parsons, pastor of the Meadow Creek
Church.

Rev. William Wheeler, stated supply of the Stites
Church.

Rev. Enoch Pond, stated supply of the North Fork Church, at the time of his death, March 20, 1907.

Rev. Silas Whitman, after a life of faithful service, died in June, 1905.

There were in all eleven native ministers, three of whom have already laid down their armour.

There are four students for the ministry at this time.

E. J. Conner and James Dickson are licensed, but not yet ordained.

Mr. and Mrs. Spalding and their helpers before the Whitman massacre were all under the American Board of Commissioners for Foreign Missions, now called the American Board. There was no Presbyterian Foreign Board at that time for them to work under, but when Mr. Spalding came back in 1871, after being absent for about twenty-four years, he returned under appointment of the Presbyterian Board of Foreign Missions. He and all the regularly commissioned missionaries who succeeded him were sent out under that board until the year 1893, when the Nez Perces mission was transferred from the Foreign to the Home Board. Mr. Spalding returned in '71, died in '74. Miss S. L. McBeth came among the Nez Perces as a teacher in the government school, in 1873, but soon after was taken under the Foreign Board.

Rev. G. L. Deffenbaugh arrived in Lapwai in the fall of 1878, and left the mission in the spring of 1888.

Kate C. McBeth arrived in the fall of 1879.

Rev. Alexander Adair came in the fall of 1893. Left the mission in October of 1896.

Mazie Crawford began the regular mission work in 1899.

Rev. Lowery Sibbet arrived the first of July, 1897, died October 16th, the same year, in Hamilton, Montana. He started out with the Nez Perces missionaries who were going among the Shoshones of Southern Idaho. Took sick there and was taken over into Montana in order to reach the railroad, one of the Nez Perces accompanying him. He really was but beginning the work when he was called to lay it down.

Rev. A. M. McLean was appointed as superintendent of the mission in the spring of 1898. He remained until the spring of 1901.

It is now thought unnecessary to have a superintendent of missions among the Nez Perces. They are doing very well alone. The services of each church are conducted with spirit and dignity. They are good singers. Perhaps hundreds of our old songs of Zion are translated and in use in their churches, and they are constantly adding thereunto. Some of the ministers and mission pupils are quite able to translate hymns. The gospel has been sung into the hearts of the Nez Perces. I have great pity for the old people of any tribe who have none of the inspiring old songs of the past ages in their own tongue. The English is always sung in Sabbath-school and Christian Endeavour, but that can only reach and touch the young.

In looking back to that old church of Waiyelatpoo, which was in reality a Nez Perces church, for the laymen were mostly of the Nez Perces tribe, I can see from that small beginning (God using the Nez Perces as instruments) has grown six churches among the Nez Perces, two among the Spokanes, one among the Umatillas, one among the Shoshones of Southern Idaho, one among the Shivwits of Utah, and we will hope another one will be set up in the region beyond, in Nevada. Our Lord hath wrought wondrously. To Him will be all the praise.

APPENDIX

How very misty Indian traditions look back of the third generation from the present, as we try to gather up the myths and customs of the past! Tradition says there was a time before the people came, that the animals represented the people and were gifted with speech. How human-like the friendships, revenges and love affairs of the animals were. The over-reaching cunningness of the coyote in particular, as well as that of his cousin, the fox, is evident in all their traditions. If you ask how long this period (before the people came) lasted, the answer is " Koon " (don't know). The coyote was constantly saying, " Na-te-tam he-wah-yam " (the people are coming). The animals began to question in their councils, " What will become of us ? " " Where will we go to ? " Answers were ready. The bear said, " I go to the mountains and hide a part of the time in a hole." The beaver said, " I can hide part of the time in the water." The birds said, " We will make our nests up so high in the branches of the trees, when the people come, they cannot get us." When the people came, the animals at once became silent. Their tradition of the animals coming first would suit Darwin.

According to the people's statements, " Tewats "

(medicine men), in former ages were skunks. The chiefs were the coyotes, and so on, they trace the different kinds of people back to the animals.

THE MYTH OF CREATION

The Kamiah Valley is celebrated for its beautiful scenery. It is named from the Kamiah Creek which enters into the Clearwater in the eastern part of the reserve. Just where the creek empties into the river, the valley is about two miles wide. Mountain ranges are on both sides of the river, not bare, steep mountains such as you might imagine, but made up of buttes (little hills), one rising back of and higher than the other, until the fifth, sixth, or seventh, with its pretty fir trees, makes heaven seem but a step farther up. Here and there a canyon divides the mountain ranges, letting the snow water out in the spring and early summer, to make its annual trip down the Clearwater, Snake and Columbia Rivers to the grand Pacific Ocean. Now here, in this beautiful valley, down by the old ferry, there is a mound, so large it looks like a hill. It is surrounded by level ground. The Nez Perces call it " The Heart " and tell the story of how it came to be there.

After the world was made, but no people yet, in Kamiah there lay a great monster. He was so large he filled the valley. That mound marks just where the heart of it was. He did not need to search for food, for he could draw in animals, great and small, for a distance of many miles, and swallow them alive. Many a council was held, at a distance, to devise some means to destroy this enemy of all beast-kind, for the valley was white with the bones of their friends. Only one among them all dared to approach the dreaded animal. This was the coyote, or the little wolf, for always, when he drew near, the creature shut his mouth tight, saying, " Go away, go away ! " One day, after the coyote had gathered some pitch-pine and flint, he crept quietly up alongside the monster, and hit the shut mouth so that it opened with a jerk, and in a moment the little brave was inside the great prison house. What a company he found there, the sick, dead, and dying ! Soon with his pitch and flint he kindled a fire, and the smoke came puffing out of the mouth, ears and nose of the monster. The little commander inside ordered all yet alive to make their escape. The great white bear said he was not able to go, but finally went out through the ear gate. All this time the coyote was sawing away on the great heart with his flint, listening with delight to the sick groans of the dying beast.

When all the captives were out and at liberty, there stood in the silence only the coyote and his friend the fox. What should be done with this great body? They finally decided to cut it in pieces, and from the pieces people the world. So the Blackfoot Indians were made from the feet, the Crows and Flatheads from the head, and other tribes were made from other parts of the body and sent off to their own lands. The two friends were left alone. The fox, looking up and down the river said, " Why, we have made no people for this beautiful valley, and nothing left to make them from." " True," said the coyote, " nothing but a few drops of the heart's best blood left on my hands. Bring me some water from the river." This was done. While the coyote washed his hands, he sprinkled the ground with blood and water, and lo ! the noble Nez Perces sprang up.

In the clear light of the Gospel, this myth looks very silly to them now, but it was fully believed in the olden time.

ALLALIMYAH

Al-la-lim-yah, the Mountain Spirit, or Spirit of the Wind, was in the form of a person, a tall, old man, taller than any tree, walking to and fro continually, never resting, never eating—wailing and weeping. Tears of blood were constantly dropping, not only from his eyes, but from the great staff which he carried in his hands. Many of the people a long time ago tried to touch his person, but found nothing in their hands but air. They could not tell whether man or woman they grasped. With his breath he started all the breezes. If he did rest a moment, it was at his turning-places. One of these was over at that mountain, " Ya-mas-tas," near Moscow. The other turning-place was near Asotin. He was on the go all the time, first one way, then turned and went back over the same road. Now that mountain, Yamastas, is where the Nez Perces took refuge at the time of the great flood (Noah's), when all other places but that one had been submerged. The stone is there yet in which they pounded their *kouse* (root for food). The people say it looks just like one of their old mortars.

Allalimyah was a great spirit, ranking higher than the Spirit of the Cold or Heat. He it was who sent the " Wy-ya-kin " in form of bird or beast, to their sons or daughters when alone on the mountains.

WYYAKIN

" Wy-ya-kin " was an attending spirit. When a child was seven, eight, or ten years old, he or she was sent off to the mountains alone, to get his or her " Wy-ya-kin," and with it a new name. The child was to remain there night as well as day—having nothing to eat—until some animal or bird would come and speak to the child. Then he was free to return. A feather of that species of bird, or a tail of the kind of animal that talked to him, was to be kept and worn throughout life as a symbol of his attending spirit. No arrow could kill him. He was invulnerable while he kept it and trusted in it.

And how they held to that feather or tail! How hard to throw it away even after the Gospel came. At the funeral of a child, the last of a family of eight girls and boys, a woman whispered to me, " We think the mother has not thrown away her Wyyakin, but is hiding it somewhere, and that is the reason her children all die."

The people tell yet how afraid they were to go alone to the mountains for their Wyyakin. This trying experience was to make them courageous also.

Al-la-lim-yah, the Spirit of the Wind, or Mountain, was all-important in this matter. He it was who sent the bird or animal to speak to the child. Sometimes from sheer exhaustion the child would fall asleep, and in his dreams would see the Wy-ya-kin. In after-life the Christian has scruples about eating his Wy-ya-kin, reminding us we need the same charity for the weak Nez Perces that Paul had for his weak brethren at Corinth—" If meat cause my brother to offend, I will eat no meat," etc.

THE MAGPIES

This was before the people came. The coyote said to his nephew, his sister's son, the fox, " I want you to run a race with five brother elks, and if you outrun them, we will cut their throats and we will have a great feast for ourselves." As the coyote was the acknowledged lawmaker, all the animals were called and took position to watch the race. From their high ground they could see if it was an honest contest. Great was the excitement—for all knew the elks were good runners. Surely, some one of the five brothers would win the race. But, no ! no ! The fox did, and did honest running—no sly outwitting either the five elks or the spectators. He reached the limit and doubled the ground with ease. The five elks were beheaded, the buffalo tent put up to smoke the venison so that nothing would be lost, and the coyote and fox had given another illustration of their authority and power over even larger animals than themselves. They rested on their honours while the stomach was comforted, but when the cravings of hunger were felt again, the coyote cast his longing eyes upon the mountain sheep, and told the fox he must run another race, with five mountain sheep (males). So the animals were called, and assembled at the call of their king, who said to the fox, " The mountain sheep is good eating. Do not be faint-hearted. Many witnesses are about you." So spake the coyote to his nephew, the fox. Off they started, but it was not long the sheep were upon the track until their friends could see they began to pant. They knew why—because they were large and fat. So one of the five sheep said—"No use trying any longer." They gave up quickly and were beheaded. The coyote and fox always carried little stone knives with them.

All was peace for a time, but that did not last very long. The next want of the coyote was for something to adorn himself with. He said to the fox, " You must run a race with five magpies. I want the wings and tails for ornaments for my head." But, " No," said the fox. " I do not want to run. The magpies are fierce. I am afraid of them although they are small." "Go, go," said the coyote. The magpies were called and all preliminaries settled for the race. The coyote had already sent for the animals to assemble. The race-track was to be up and back a precipitous mountain, so for better position, many of the animals perched themselves on the crest of the mountain. All started off. The coyote, of course, was at the bottom, awaiting results, knife in hand. Not much betting on the magpies as they watched the fox gracefully climb from rock to rock, but as they began to descend, the magpies surprised their friends by clapping their wings tight to their sides and holding them there. Down they went, like a canoe running the rapids. At the bottom, the fox found the victorious magpies waiting to take his head off. He plead, " O, let me dip myself in the brook and cool myself before I die." So down he ran and hid himself in the bushes and under the roots in the water. But the magpies' sharp eyes found him—jerked him out and killed him. It had not turned out as the coyote had expected, and he was nowhere in sight when the end came.

MYTH OF THE SEASONS

When the clouds from the Northeast met the clouds from the Southwest, they mingled as if fighting. When "Youn," or Cold, is not so strong as

" Lo-ki-ye-wah," Heat, then the Chinook wind prevails. A long time ago the five sons of Youn, " Halp Halp," and the five sons of Lo-ki-ye-wah, " Te-kits-e-yah," met and fought a long time. The children of Lo-ki-ye-wah were all killed but one daughter. She was with child. She returned towards the South where she lived in her little tent. Her child was born, a son. She cared for him well, constantly telling him of the enmity between Youn, the Cold, and Lo-ki-ye-wah, the Heat. When that son grew up, he came as far north as the eastern side of The Dalles. There he met the grandchildren of Youn. There was a frozen sea there then. They fought on ice. Youn got wooden vessels of grease and spread it on the ice. Lokiyewah poured warm water on it. They still fought although the ice was crushing under them. The coyote, boss of all, appeared upon the scene and cut the throat of Lokiyewah, saying, " From this time onward it shall not always be cold, neither shall it be always warm. Part of the time it shall be warm and part of the time cold." So the seasons were settled.

This myth is so well known that in the spring-time, when the high winds of the mountains prevail, the people say, " Youn is not killed yet. The fight is going on. Lokiyewah is strong and will conquer, if spring-time. In the fall, Youn grows the stronger." This battle was fought just before the people came. The animals have had nothing to say since. Chinook was a people, the people of the warm wind.

The Myth of the Mountain Sheep

There were five brothers, mountain sheep. The oldest one had a wife and child, but somehow he was not contented. He wandered away. He killed a deer, ate some and went to sleep. In some way he had hurt his hand, and in his sleep he sucked some of the blood from it. He waked up and thought how good that tasted. "What is there around here so good!" He searched but found nothing. Then somehow he tasted the blood from his own hand again and thought it was delicious. So he cut off the calf of his leg and ate it. He wanted more, so cut off a piece from the other leg. Then he thought, "I look awful. I can never go back among my friends again. If I could just walk around in the water it would not be noticed." Then he cut off more and more from his body. He loved it so. He even cut off a little bit of his own tongue and ate that.

The brother next to him became uneasy at his long absence and started out to hunt him up, calling every once in a while his name. At last he answered. The brother said, "Come here to me." He said, "I cannot, a stick is run through me, and I cannot move. You come to me." So the brother approached him. He took a long rope made of the entrails of the deer, wound it up and threw it as a lasso. He caught his brother by the foot, drew him up to him, cut him up and ate him. There was nothing left but his bones.

A third brother became uneasy about the two

brothers. He came like the other one, calling as he walked along. He was answered in the same way and told the same thing. "I have got a stick in me. I cannot move. You come to me." So the brother approached, was caught by the foot in the same way, was eaten, piece by piece, and enjoyed.

Some time afterwards, the fourth brother, with care-worn heart, went out to search for these missing ones. The same thing happened. He was caught and eaten just as the others had been.

The fifth brother started, and as he was going along the trail he stepped on a meadow lark and broke its leg. "Oh! me!" said the meadow lark, "what will become of me now? I cannot walk." The mountain sheep brother said, "I will fix your leg and make it whole, if you will tell me about my brothers." So the meadow lark gave him the full particulars, and put him on his guard. She told him to stick arrows all over himself, so that when the lasso was thrown, it would be cut. So he got himself ready. The brother called him. He approached, and the lasso was thrown as before, but this time, it gave way. The fifth brother hastened home and told the coyote all about it.

The coyote said to his friends, "We will leave this place. We do not want him coming back among us. We are afraid of him." He said to the man's wife, "You come along, too." But she said, "No, I will stay here. You are not my man, and I will not go away." They all went off and left her and her baby there alone. She lived by the Clearwater, in Kamiah. Now as she sat there one day she heard some one singing. She listened, and knew the voice. It was her husband. He had made up his mind to return home. So he got himself ready. He gathered up the bones of his brothers, tied them together with the piece of the lasso, threw them over his shoulder and started. As he came along he thought of the five beautiful maidens of Cœur d'Alene and began mournfully to sing, " What will the five beautiful maidens of the Cœur d'Alene say when they hear I have killed my brothers ! What will the five beautiful maidens of the Cœur d'Alene say when they hear I have killed my brothers !" He was singing it over and over again and the bones were rattling on his back.

His wife listened, and was not so brave as when the people left her. He came to her door, threw down the bones, and entered. She knew what it meant. She was nursing the baby. He took the baby from her and sat down. He began dandling it on his knees and singing, " Oh ! my child, I will eat you. Oh ! my child, I will eat you."

Then she was afraid and thought quickly of what she could do. She hid a big horn spoon under her arm as she stirred about, and then said to him, " Just give me the child for a little while. It is not clean. I will take it to the brook and wash it in honour of your home-coming." He was not willing at first, but she said so many nice things about making the child nice and clean in his honour, that at last he gave it to her and told her to be quick about it.

She hurried down to the river and told the willow on the bank to cry like a child, and when he called to answer—" In a little while I will be ready," and then to keep on crying like a child. She put her spoon into the river, and lo ! it became a canoe. So off she went up the river to where the coyote and her friends were, and told them. Then Mo-ki, the crane, said, " If you will do as I say, I will kill him when he comes. Just bury me,—right on the side of the hill (by Isaac's, it was), face to the river, with one leg straight down and the other bent." They did so. Only covered the body, but the legs could be seen.

Pretty soon along came the old brother. He turned the corner and saw the body, and said, " Oh ! are you dead ! " So he put the bones down and went sighting around, and began to cut away at Mo-ki's leg. He meant to eat it. As he was stooping down, Mo-ki kicked out the bent leg hard, and hit the old fellow and he went all to pieces. He was about all gone anyway.

The Nez Perces think this myth contains good teaching. They use it to illustrate the course of the gambler and drunkard. I suppose they would say the bones he carried around with him meant remorse. They say when a man drinks and gambles, he eats himself, wife, children and all his friends.

Names

The child did not receive its name until six, seven, or eight years old. Up to that time it had some pet name, as " My child," " My darling." Then the Spirit of the Wind, " Al-la-lim-yah," gave the child a name. So the first names were all given by him. In after generations the boy was called, usually, after the father's people—the girl, after the mother's. If there was any debate about the child's name, whether it should be called after the father or the mother, the people settled it at the next Feast of the Dead—by father or mother taking something there, such as a blanket. After the distribution of all that belonged to the dead was made, the parent would hold up the gift, or show it, announce the name, and say, " I wish my child's name to be ————." An old man or woman would say, " Aah," then all would say, " Aah." Thus assent was given. The gift was laid down for any one to take up. The child after that was called by that name.

Sometimes in after-life a person rejected the name by which he was called and wanted it changed. He could go through the same process—make a present at a gathering and the people's consent would change it.

Men's names were from the large birds, and fierce animals. Women's names from the lesser animals and birds, or from the land. If from the land, it has the suffix " mah" or " my." All tribes used such names as Bear, Wolf, Goose, Eagle, for men's names.

The coyote is in evidence all through Nez Perces traditions, proclaiming himself at all times to be invulnerable. " I may be killed or drowned twenty times, but still I live." He was the chief of the larger animals. " Al-le-tup-nin," the mink, chief of the smaller, furred animals.

Original names were from " Al-la-yim-yah," Spirit of the Wind ; " Ah-lew-yah," Winter ; " Lo-ki-ye-wah," Heat. Any variations in meaning were usually made by the addition of suffixes to this root.

Chief names were from large birds, beasts and the sun. No names from the moon. Moon is simply the son of the Night. Sometimes children or people were given names from some striking peculiarity seen about them, as " Timps-te-te-lew," large cherries. (Her eyes looked like them.) " Hin-ma-toun-se-lu," the lightning's eyes. There were many outlandish names with seemingly no reason for them.

They had a vague idea of a place of sorrow, where the bad spirits were. There was no talk of the Happy Hunting Ground.

BURIAL CUSTOMS

When any one dies, a rider is sent all around to say, " Now ———— sleeps."

Sometimes there are those who would like to stand and talk a little to the departed one, then bow the head as if bidding the dear one " good-bye." Even

yet, at times the minister will say, " Do not bow your
head. The soul has gone. Only the outside case lies
before you."

The heathen show their sorrow by dishevelled locks,
and untidy appearance, while telling over the many
good qualities of their friend.

They used to bury many things with the dead.
Some few will even yet drop in a blanket or a dress
which had been worn by the departed. It is only a
very few of the heathen who bury as they used to.
They may have a medicine man drumming around
the sick and dying, but when all is over, they want a
Christian burial.

They give all the things belonging to the dead
away—privately, if Christians ; in a most public manner, if heathen. This public gathering we call the
Feast of the Dead. It is very hard to break up this
old custom. Of course each one has a curiosity to
see what he will get.

In the very olden times, they piled stones over a
shallow grave. There was such a thing as burying
alive. They tell of a father—very old—who got down
in his son's grave and was actually buried. He did
not want to live any longer.

Another story is told of a man who said he must be
buried with his friend, but when they went to push him
in, he jumped across and got away.

They used to burn or tear down the houses of the
dead. That, of course, is broken up, but I see they

just a little prefer to live somewhere else for a little time. They are children of Nature and love to carry out their impulses. The desolate, lonely place is too much for them.